Where Memories Were Made

Stories by an Oregon Hunter

by

Charles Sharps

Trafford Publishing

Order this book online at www.trafford.com
or email orders@trafford.com

Most Trafford titles are also available at major online book retailers.

Printed in Victoria, BC, Canada.

ISBN: 978-1-4269-2392-0 (sc)
ISBN: 978-1-4269-2393-7 (dj)

Library of Congress Control Number: 2009914036

*Our mission is to efficiently provide the world's finest, most comprehensive book publishing
service, enabling every author to experience success. To find out how to publish your
book, your way, and have it available worldwide, visit us online at www.trafford.com*

Trafford rev. 2/01/2010

www.trafford.com

North America & international
toll-free: 1 888 232 4444 (USA & Canada)
phone: 250 383 6864 ✦ fax: 812 355 4082

DEDICATION

To my wife of 40 years Sue, and sons John and Joe whose support and companionship made these stories possible, and to Riley and Dylan sons of my son John.

ACKNOWLEDGEMENTS

Thanks to Kathy Erickson for her encouragement and editorial skills, and to Sally Harrold for her instruction and editing on the finer aspects of writing. And further thanks to all whom, after reading my memoir on Nam pushed me to complete this collection of short stories.

TABLE OF CONTENTS

BLACKPOWDER ELK

It was with a strong sense of disappointment that I backed my truck out of the garage and headed towards Dishner's for breakfast. I had waited six months for black powder antlerless elk season to begin and today was opening day. My rifle, a .50 caliber Thompson Center was sighted in. I could hit targets at 100 yards. I knew where the elk were, and my hunting partners were all physically fit.

I was disappointed because it was foggy and raining hard. The rain I could live with, but I have never found a way to spot game in the fog.

By the time I arrived at Dishner's, to meet my hunting partners, Richard Spring and Jack Fearell, it was raining so hard I got drenched running the 50 feet or so to the door. "Why m++e, Lord?" I asked, as I scooted through the door. "Why couldn't today have been as clear and sunny as yesterday? Oh well, "I mused, just a little reality check." I would have fun keeping my powder and caps dry.

Over breakfast, my hunting partners and I discussed our hunting options and decided we should return to the Benson Creek area where we had scouted a small herd the previous weekend. I was the only hunter with a tag and they were along to dog for me as I had helped them during the regular bull elk season.

Leaving Dishners, I was glad to see the rain had slackened

and hoped it would stop. The weatherman had promised partial clearing for the afternoon, but anything is possible on the Oregon Coast.

Taking two trucks, Jack and I headed north for our 20-minute drive into some of the finest elk country in Oregon. We would be hunting in the Elliot State Forest, a land of steep hills, large clearcuts, and home to thousands of elk.

Rendezvousing on Benson Ridge with Rick (who had stopped to pick up his 8- year old son, Justin) we put on our foul-weather gear. Our gear is made by Filson and is known by local hunters and loggers, individuals who live outdoors during Oregon's rainy season as tin pants and jackets. They are made from heavy, wax-impregnated cotton, and are indestructible which is why it is called tin. We also wear leather, high-topped caulked boots, because the terrain is so steep they are a safety factor when it comes to scrambling up and down the very steep hills.

Heading for the timber, we quickly picked up fresh elk sign heading up what we call Salmon Ridge. We had not expected them to be going up. (Didn't they know they were supposed to head down?) Altering our game plan, it was decided I would drive around to the top of Salmon Ridge and attempt to get in front of the herd, while Rick and Jack tracked them.

It was a 40-minute walk back to my truck, a 20- minute drive and another 15- minute walk before I got into position where I hoped the elk would pass. The rain had slackened, the fog was gone on top of the ridge, but I could not see into the valley below. I had waited approximately an hour and a half when I spotted Jack and Rick laboriously climbing up through the timber following the elk trail. Obviously, they had gone through before I could get in front of them.

Talking quietly, it was decided I would track the herd, as Jack, Rick and Justin attempted to get ahead of them with the hope of turning them back. Maybe we could catch them in a squeeze.

It did not work.

Following the tracks, they slowly swung to the east and- you guessed it- went back to the bottom only yards from where we had originally picked up their tracks. I followed them down Salmon Ridge and along Benson Creek for mile or so and they never stopped. They were headed for another ridge top in the opposite direction of my partners and I did not want to be that deep into the timber without some extra help. Slowly I retraced the trail I had followed to the bottom reaching the top and my partners; rather tuckered out from all my climbing.

Stopping for lunch, we decided to drive further into the Elliot State Forest hoping to see if we could spot other elk feeding in the clear cuts. After lunch, we drove about five miles and spotted six cows and a spike feeding in a clearcut. It was decided the best way to approach without spooking them, was to sneak through the timber hoping to get within the 100 yards or so before I attempted a shot. This hunt failed. When Jack and I approached the area, all we found were fresh tracks, dingle berries (elk droppings) and the strong smell of elk. The tracks indicated this particular bunch also headed out and down for the sanctuary of the timber and none of us wanted a shoot–and-pack show.

It was getting early on in the afternoon. It gets dark around 4:30 and there are literally hundreds of elk in this part of Oregon if you know where to look. It was easier to attempt to find another herd or come back the next day and try again. Roosevelt elk will not travel very far if they are not pushed. We are all successful elk hunters and we have all killed elk in the deepest of canyons where it takes two or three days to pack them out by packboard. (This country is too steep for a pack horse).

Climbing back up to our rigs, we decided to give it one more try, for who knew in what clearcut we might not spot more elk? Luck was with us, for we had not traveled more than a mile when four more cows were spotted feeding about halfway up the side of a huge rectangular-shaped clear cut. We stopped to glass to insure none were bulls or cows with calves. As we glassed, the sun came out. "Maybe this is a good sign," I thought.

We agreed that the big old lead cow would be the one I would attempt to shoot. Fatigue forgotten, I quickly climbed a ridge, circling the herd getting above and behind the cows, which put me between them and the timber. My partners stayed on the other side of the clearcut conveying by hand signals where I was to stalk. I was in heavy greasewood and small fir trees and about the only way I could see them was to get up on an old stump and check them out with my binoculars.

The cows heard me thrashing through the greasewood, spooked, and headed for the bottom. I heard them go and started to get frustrated, it was impossible to see. What had appeared to be open country from the other side of the clearcut was head high brush interspersed with small fir trees.

I found a small clearing with a stump which allowed me an excellent view of the far side. Jack signaled they had gone down and where up on his side, glassing I attempted to spot them but couldn't. "How can such huge animals hide so easily?" I wondered.

Suddenly, there she was my lead cow headed to the top. Too far to shoot was my first thought, my second was shoot now or she is going to get even further in a matter of seconds.

Sighting over the top of the stump I set the trigger on my .50 caliber Hawkins and touched the set trigger only to hear `click'. Desperately I flipped off the damp cap and replaced it with another, sighting carefully on my now standing elk, I again touched the front trigger and again heard the familiar `click'.

I was so frustrated because my rifle would not fire; I deliberated throwing my rifle off the hill. The caps were damp from all the rain. Angry and frustrated forcing myself to calm down, I placed a third cap on the nipple, took a deep breath and gently stroked the front trigger.

KA-BOOM the rifle roared and a huge cloud of white smoke completely obliterated my target. Jumping up on the stump, I saw my cow falling back down towards the bottom and I knew she was dead.

Dancing a jig on top of the stump I let out a war hoop that was heard for miles, I had just killed my first elk with-one good shot-and with a black powder rifle.

WHAT HAPPENS AFTER
ONE GOOD SHOT?

Sighting over the top of the stump, I carefully set the rear trigger on my .50 caliber Thompson and lightly squeezed the set trigger only to hear click. Desperately, I flipped off the damp cap and replaced it with another. Sighting carefully on my now standing elk, I again touched the front trigger and again heard the familiar click.

I almost pitched my rifle off the hill; I was so frustrated and angry.

Taking several deep breaths in order to calm my nerves, I placed a third cap on the nipple, took another a deep breath and gently stroked the front trigger. KABOOM! The rifle roared and a huge cloud of white smoke completely obliterated my target. Jumping up on the stump to get out of the smoke, I saw my cow elk falling back down toward the bottom and I knew she was dead. Dancing a jig on top of the stump, I let out a war hoop that could have been heard for miles, I had just killed my first elk with a black powder rifle and with one good shot.

It was 2:30 in the afternoon. It would be dark by 4:45, and I had just killed a 500- pound animal in some of the steepest terrain the Oregon Coast range has to offer. How was I going to get it out of the woods? It was approximately 800 yards almost straight up the side of a ridge to a road that would be passable to a four-wheel-drive truck, if I could get the elk to the truck.

I had several options: I could quarter the elk, which really means cutting into eighths and pack it out on my back. I could bone it, that is remove all the meat from the bone and then carry it out. I could use a chainsaw winch and drag it out whole, or use the power winch on my truck if I had enough line to reach.

But first, I had to get to my elk and gut it. Climbing down the side of my ridge heading for the bottom where my elk slid when it died was difficult, because of the steep terrain. Approaching the bottom, I had to detour downstream about 100 yards because the walls had turned to rock. It was difficult to get to, but not impossible and I soon reached the bottom. Walking upstream, my decision as to the method of removal was soon made for me. She had dropped on her stomach, effectively damming the creek and water was already starting to pool behind her. I knew it would be impossible to move her, I tried anyway but I could not. She was effectively lodged in a mini-canyon, with rock walls about 40 feet high. My decision became simple: Get some sort of line and winch her out. I rejected boning and quartering, due to the difficulty of the situation, pooling water, rock walls, and steepness of the terrain. Climbing high enough so I could holler to my hunting partners, Rick Spring, his son, Justin; and my brother-in-law, Jack Fearell, I explained "our" predicament. Rick, Jack and Justin hiked back to Rick's truck because it had a machete, haywire, packboards and a power winch. I never hunt alone and if I had been, it would have been almost impossible for me to get my elk out. Leaving our elk I climbed back to the top of my ridge and hiked to my truck where I could secure my rifle, binoculars and other hunting gear. We had agreed to meet on the road above the elk as soon as we could. It was now 3:30.

If it were not for my hunting partners, I probably would still be in the bottom of the canyon living off elk jerky. We gathered on the road above our elk about 4. We had gear, food, and clothing to spend the night if we had to, but decided it would not be necessary.

We decided we had enough haywire and winch line to reach the elk from the truck. All we had to do was get it attached and pull her out. We had discussed using the chainsaw winch, but the trees were not large enough to get a good toehold for pulling. Rick grabbed the machete and started cutting a path straight down the mountain, while Jack and I struck out ahead, each carrying two large rolls of haywire over our shoulders. At various points along the way, we would stop and holler back to Rick, in order for him to maintain the straight path we needed for winching. We also dropped three sections of the wire to be strung later.

Tying the end of the last section to a small tree, Jack and I proceeded the final distance to the elk, having to throw the line down the last 40 feet as we looked for a way down. Reaching the elk, we put a loop around her neck with a half hitch on her nose which would hold her head up when we started winching. It was almost dark and we had not moved her an inch. Jack stayed with the elk as I proceeded back up the mountain to help Rick cut the trail and to attach all four sections of haywire.

I had climbed so often and was some what dehydrated, so my thighs started to cramp and I had to stop every 10 feet or so to catch my breath and rest my legs. Forty minutes after leaving Jack, I was back on the road getting a flashlight and grabbing the end of the winch line off the truck. Back down the mountain I went, meeting Rick on his way back up after having blazed a trail clear to the bottom.

We had decided earlier Rick would run the controls on the winch, Justin and I would relay directions and Jack would guide the elk. Pulling the cable off the winch, we found we were approximately eight feet short of connecting the four sections of wire to the truck. It was back up the mountain in the dark (I had fallen and broken the light) to get a short chain in order to make the reach.

Jack was alone; in the dark; sitting on an elk without a clue as to what was going on, or why it was taking so long. My legs were killing me by the time I got back up to the road, but Rick had a chain ready and off I went, back down. The moon was now high enough to provide illumination to see the path and the haywire as it lay glistening in its light. Connecting the winch line to the haywire only took a few minutes before I hollered to Jack, "Are you ready?" There was no response. I yelled a half a dozen times and the only one who heard me were Rick and Justin. I would have to go farther down the mountain to see what was wrong with Jack.

All sorts of weird ideas floated through my mind as I went back down. "He's had a heart attack." "Rolling rocks from the hillside hit him on the head and he is unconscious." "Maybe the elk jumped up and trampled him."

I knew that was dumb, but I was worried.

As I neared the bottom, I gave another yell, and was happy to hear a response. It turns out the creek was making so much noise he just could not hear me and now another problem. From my position lower down the mountain, Rick could hear, but he could not understand.

Back up the mountain I went just far enough for our relay to work and, for the first time I hours, I believed we were going to get the elk out without having to spend the night. It was now 7:30.

With the haywire grinding on the rock cliff, our elk slowly started to move. Jack's job was to insure she would not get hung up on small trees, roots or stumps. That would certainly guarantee a broken line. He did this by continually pulling at the wire attached to her nose, continually lifting the head as she slid upward. He could not do this going up the initial 40 feet, but this proved to be one of the easiest parts. It was all rock, straight up and nothing for her to hang up on. Pulling on the wire is backbreaking work. Imagine picking up a 50 pound load every 20 seconds or so for 30 minutes or more and you have some idea of the labor involved.

From my position, I watched one section of haywire go by and could hear Jack huffing and puffing and he pulled on the wire. We were continually hollering, "Whoop" (a logging term meaning stop) or "Ho! Ho!" (meaning go). You can not confuse the two, they sound so different. Confusion is the last thing you want when pulling an animal this size out of the woods. About 8, Jack reached my position and it was my turn to pull and guide the haywire. Jack went on ahead to help Rick and Justin, who were taking line off the winch as fast as it was coming in.

Slowly we moved upward, I lost track of the amount of times I whooped, to stop the winch as I cleared some obstacle out of the path. My legs were killing me, and it was with a great effort, I kept myself from just riding the elk to the top. The last section of haywire had gone through the winch. We were within 100 yards of the top. The time: 8:45. The winch was getting hot, the battery was getting low, and it was necessary to stop awhile for them to cool and recharge.

It was 9:15.

I was sitting in the moonlight, as things cooled and recharged. I was exhausted, the exhilaration of a killing an elk with black powder muzzle loader was long gone. All I wanted to do was get to the top. I knew our families would be frantic. We should have been home hours ago.

Rick hollered, "Ho! Ho!" and we started moving again. I could see the lights from the truck and the shadows cast by Rick, Jack and Justin as they passed in front of the headlights. What a beautiful sight! Slowly, our elk eased onto the road, as I collapsed, legs quivering, exhausted, knowing at last, the really hard work was over.

SNAKE RIVER -
PINE CREEK, BEAR HUNT

The Snake River, Pine Creek hunting area is two units bordering the world-renowned Snake River in Eastern Oregon. It is as far east from my home on the Pacific coast as one can get and still remain in Oregon.

These hunting units contain towns, mountains and rivers with names found in Oregon's history books. Names such as Wallowa, Imnaha, Joseph, Hat Point, Freeze Out, Eagle Cap Wilderness, Richland and Halfway.

Names that tell a story of roaring streams, huge salmon, majestic elk, full curl sheep, hardy settlers, the Nez Perce tribe and Chief Joseph. The Chief Joseph who took on the entire United States Army by leaving the reservation and attempting to lead his people to freedom in Canada. After months of running, hiding, and fighting he surrendered to General Howard just twenty miles from the Canadian border. The Chief Joseph who, with tears in his voice, spoke these powerful words, "I will fight no more forever."

This story actually started last fall when my youngest son, Joe, suggested we (his brother John and I) apply for a spring bear tag in eastern Oregon. He had said that some of the best bear hunting in the state was to be had in two units called, SnakeRiver /Pine Creek.

We all applied because the success rate for drawing was

supposed to be 70%. In February we learned John and I had been successful, so we made plans to go as late in May as possible. Assuming the later in the year, the warmer the weather.

The spring bear season lasts one month in Oregon. Sows with cubs, less than one year old, are not considered fair game so we were hoping for a huge spring boar.

Joe, the one who suggested we try Eastern Oregon, works for someone who regularly and successfully makes this spring bear hunt. There was no doubt in my mind that had convinced him this was the place to go.

I was not particularly fond of the idea of driving 12 hours one way just to hunt bear. Coos County where I reside has almost as many bear as it does any other game animal. There are fantastic hunting opportunities just 15 minutes from my front door. Why drive 12 hours when 15 minutes will do?

"Because it will be fun," my wife, Sue, said. "You and the boys will get a chance to visit and have a good time, you know, male bonding."

"Who can argue with such logic?" Not me, so I quit bemoaning the time, distance and money necessary to make this a successful hunt and entered somewhat half-heartily into the planning and preparation.

Backpacking was the word the boys kept using.

"Dad, we are going to have to back pack several miles off the beaten path in order to be successful."

"We can all carry MRE's (meals ready to eat), in order to cut down on weight," said one. "We have all the light weight gear we need to stay warm and dry in the winter," he continued.

They must think I am getting old and forgetful. After all who knew better than the guy who bought all their stuff what they had for backpacking.

"Do you think you are up to it?" asked another.

"Sure," I responded. "Anywhere you can pack and walk, I can."

Didn't they know the Wallowa Mountains in May have snow on them, lots of deep, cold, wet and white snow, I wondered?

Didn't they know that sleeping on the ground for a year in Vietnam had cured me forever of sleeping bags, air mattresses and freeze-dried foods?

"Oh well, in for a penny in for a pound," my Welsh grandfather used to say, so I joined in with all the excitement I could muster.

We picked the next to last weekend of the season and took two days vacation time with the weekend. The plan was to drive one long day and hunt as much as we could for three.

I borrowed my brother-in-law Jack's pack frame and gaiters, Tracker Dave's 0- degree sleeping bag, purchased a case of MRE'S and scrupulously followed the list of needed items prepared by son John.

The living room started filling up with pack frames, lightweight sleeping bags, compasses, canteens, matches, candles, first aid kit, gortex gear, Danner boots, mess kits, etc. You name it; we had it on our list.

I even borrowed a camper shell to put on the back of my ¾ ton Ford diesel pickup to protect our gear while in route and to provide a bed for someone to rest on while driving.

Deciding which guns to take was easy.

We are all handgun hunters and Contenders were the choice for John and me. I opted to carry my 14-inch .405 Winchester and John his .375 JD Jones. Joe carried his Ruger Blackhawk in .45 Colt.

A couple of weeks before departure I started watching the paper for the weather. The long range forecast was always wet, with rain at the lower elevations and snow at the higher elevations.

We all studied topographical maps, called ranger stations and read articles on the best places to hunt. By the time we were finished with our research we decided we would hunt the North Pine Creek area in the mountains above Halfway.

Querying Internet's long range weather did little to allay my concerns, We were going to be spending a long wet weekend in the wilds of Oregon's Wallowa's.

Finally, after months of preparation I left work Wednesday afternoon around 2:00 p.m. headed for Eugene, Oregon to pick up Joe as soon as he got off work. From Eugene, Joe and I went to Corvallis to pick up John.

The truck was loaded with our gear including three huge pack frames, water, tarps, tools, and other miscellaneous gear and a large air mattress complete with blankets and pillow if someone should choose to sleep.

Our plans were to drive to LaGrande hoping to arrive by midnight. An early departure would put us into hunting country by Thursday afternoon.

After refueling, we left Corvallis around 6:30 with John resting in the back of the truck. By the time we hit the freeway 20 minutes later, he appeared to be fast asleep.

Setting the cruise control at 70 miles per hour we headed North on I-5 passing through Albany, Salem and countless small towns scattered along the freeway. We went around Portland on I-205 and picked up I-84 for the shot straight east. According to our time frame we were on target to get to LaGrande by midnight.

It was raining when I left Coos Bay and it was still raining six hours later when we stopped in the Columbia Gorge to stretch our legs.

John, asleep in the back never stirred.

Passing through Hood River, The Dalles, Rufus, Arlington, Boardman, and Stanfield, it continued to rain and I had to continually throttle back to avoid hydroplaning on the water-soaked slick highway.

Stopping to refuel and to change drivers in Pendleton, I figured we were about 30 minutes behind schedule. Pulling out of Pendleton, Joe was driving and I was comfortably bedded in the back.

I must have dozed, because it seemed only minutes had passed before we were driving down the main street of LaGrande looking for the budget motel where we had reservations.

It was probably a good thing it was 12:45 in the morning, as we unpacked the truck to secure some valuable items in the motel room. It wasn't the gear we were concerned about, it was the firearms. Our modest collection included the following: two Ruger 10-22's, one .45 acp Auto Ordinance, one AMT .45 acp Backup, one S&W K 22, one .45 Colt Ruger Blackhawk and the Contenders. There are some benefits to living in Oregon. The motel clerk never batted an eye as we walked past her armed to the teeth to our second-story room.

The beds were hard, and the idea of enjoying the advertised

continental breakfast as well as the rush to get into our hunting area had us up and on the road by 6:30. Unfortunately the coffee was weak and packaged doughnuts were stale but we were on the road. It wasn't raining, and we were looking forward to an afternoon of hunting bear.

In the distance we could see the snow capped peaks of the Wallowa's. Each peak had a belt of clouds encircling its waist giving the illusion of comfort and stability.

To get to our planned unit on the North Fork of Pine Creek we had to go to Halfway via Richland. Unfortunately it started to rain and the snow capped peaks disappeared for the rest of the trip.

In Halfway, we visited the Ranger station and asked for some advice about where to hunt. We were told the road to Imnaha had just been opened by snowplows and that the North Fork area was an excellent place to hunt.

A ranger passing through the office overheard our conversation and said to the clerk "Did you tell them there aren't any bear this time of year? And if there were, all this snow and rain would have driven them back into hibernation."

I wasn't sure if he was kidding and at the same time I vaguely remembered some old biology lessons, which seemed to indicate bear will return to their dens for another couple of weeks. Then again, I may have had bear confused with Punxsutawney Bill the ground hog.

Leaving Halfway after visiting a small gun store and getting some more advice from the proprietor about places to hunt along Big Pine Creek, we headed up into the Wallowa's.

Within minutes we were engulfed in rain and dense fog. As we climbed up and along-side the creek we attempted to take several side roads hoping to find clear cuts where we could sit and glass for foraging bear. Unfortunately, the side roads dead ended out in the middle of nowhere or were blocked with snow drifts

Glassing is the accepted and usually the most successful method of finding bear out feeding on wild onions and other fresh greens.

By the time we got to the top of the pass between Halfway and Imnaha it was so foggy, I had turned on the truck lights.

Spotting a sign that said Hells Canyon Overlook, we pulled in for a break and to discuss our hunting plans. The overlook was so foggy, if there had not been a paved trail I am not sure I could have made the 50 yards back to my truck.

We decided after much discussion our best bet would be to forget hunting Big Pine Creek and head towards Imnaha and Freeze Out Trail Head where we would leave our truck and pack into the wilderness.

It was 37 miles to Imnaha and at 15 to 20 miles an hour the trip seemed to take forever. Naturally, meaning the way our luck was running, we missed the road to Freeze Out and ended up on the main street of Imnaha.

The road signs in town pointed out the directions; Hat Point Trail Head 29 miles (road not maintained in the winter), Halfway 68 miles (the way we had come), Joseph 37 miles and nothing for Freeze Out.

It is hard to disappear in a town with a dozen or so houses but my sons were gone by the time I had the truck turned around and parked. I later found out John had gone to the post office and Joe to a building with a café sign hanging out front. Obviously the closed sign on the front door did not mean anything to him because he was talking with the owner trying to get her to sell him a late lunch. But she wouldn't, telling him to come back in six months and she would be happy to sell to him.

I found John in the post office smooth talking the clerk who appeared to be all aflutter that two nice men, one young, were in her post office.

Here we learned that we had to go back down the road we had just traveled for 13 miles to find the road to Freeze Out.

Leaving the post office to cries of good luck, we headed towards the only other commercial appearing building, one with a sign that said Groceries--Tavern.

Opening the door was as though we had stepped back 50 years in time. There were a half-dozen people eating at two different tables. The rest were covered with soiled dishes. Conversations stopped instantly and every eye became focused on us. These people were locals. All were dressed in jeans, cowboy boots and wearing cowboy hats.

"Hmmm" I mused, "Guess there must be strangers in town."

We had gone into the store to replenish our snack supply, but the fact it was also a café meant I was not going to get my boys out of there without feeding them.

It took the waitress awhile but she finally arrived with menus and after clearing a table we were not using, suggested we come to it and order because the service would be faster and would make her life easier.

We moved and ordered cheeseburgers and fries.

The food was good

Halfway through our meal, John spotted a Forest Service truck parking out front and went out to inquire as to the condition of the road to Hat Point. The ranger said he didn't know and directed John to one of the locals who said he thought the road was blocked with snow at the 15-mile point.

As we munched on fries and debated our next move, the local patrons finished eating and as they slowly walked past looked us over as though we were on exhibition. No one nodded and said hi or good luck.

Within an hour of arriving in Imnaha, we were headed back down the road to find Freeze Out trail head. Before leaving I had called home and left a message as to where we could be found.

Right where the postmistress said it would be, a road with a small hand- lettered sign that said, "Freeze Out." No wonder we had missed it coming the other way, it was so small we almost missed it while knowing where to look.

As we started up the steep gravel road it started to rain. Shifting into four-wheel drive to avoid beating up my truck, I remarked, "We are lucky it isn't snowing."

The trailhead was a short two miles up the road and in the parking lot were 14 horse trailers. Two were loaded and leaving.

Once again we debated parking and hiking in to make camp. But we did not want to follow the muddy trail the horses had made and compete with so many other different bear hunters.

Hat Point became our next objective.

Returning back to Imnaha, I again called home and again left instructions as to where we would be hunting.

There was a 15 percent grade sign at the beginning of the road as well as others saying narrow one lane road, use pullouts etc. A

15 percent road grade is steep. Most major paved highways are constructed to avoid anything over 6 percent. Shifting back into four wheel drive because the road was slippery from the continual rain, made the climb rather pleasant and for the first time we were in prime bear country.

We could see for miles and miles vast green hills just begging to be trodden upon by a bear. We assumed this panorama would go on forever but it wasn't too long, about 8 miles up the road, when we headed back into the timber.

Knowing there were green vistas and good hunting behind us, we decided to follow the road to Hat Point just to see what was out there.

As we climbed higher, the rain turned to snow and the ponderosa pines looked like a Christmas post card. The road rapidly turned white and still we pressed on. Soon we were driving through snowdrifts packed hard as ice. At the 15-mile point I started getting nervous and told the boys it would be prudent to turn around and make camp back where we had spent a few minutes glassing for bear.

I also told them a story about some hunters who had frozen to death because they just wanted to drive a little farther and had become stuck in the snow. They had not reported their destination to anyone, rescuers never looked in their area and they had been found the following spring frozen in their mired truck.

My story had the desired effect and they agreed it would be a good idea to turn around.

After turning around we went back several miles and picked up a very rough spur road we had noticed earlier. Following it for several miles through open range and patches of timber we stopped to camp.

Camp was set up in driving rain. I started a fire, as the boys strung a huge 16 x 20-foot tarp among four convenient trees and pitched their tent. We utilized a second tarp as a wall, which kept the wind off the fire. Before we were finished the rain stopped, the sun came out and our moods changed from one of weariness and dejection to laughter and high hopes.

We scouted the territory for several hours before dark, looking for bear sign and opportunities to sit and glass in the morning.

We found some tracks but what disturbed me a little was the huge snowdrifts on the northern side of all the gullies and draws.

We were further up in the mountains than I wanted to be.

Returning to camp just before dark, we feasted on Van Camp pork and beans, bagels, and cups of hot chocolate.

By 9 o'clock, it was so cold we decided to go to bed in order to get warm. John and Joe were going to sleep in the tent and I was bunking in the back of my pickup.

We all had cold-weather gear, our sleeping bags were rated for 0 degrees and our tarp was pitched for rain, and we had gathered a huge pile of dried wood for a breakfast fire in the morning.

Soon we were all as snug as the proverbial bugs in a rug.

At 1 a.m. I got up to go to the bathroom. It was very cold, the fog so thick I could hardly see the boys tent. It was quiet and dark, the air felt eerily still and ominous. Returning to bed I shivered and shook until I warmed up and started to doze.

About 1:30, the wind came up with a roar and solid ice pelted the fiberglass shell of my camper so loudly I thought it might crack. Fumbling for my flashlight I could see by the light shining through their tent that the boys were awake.

"Go back to bed," I hollered. "There isn't anything we can do until the morning."

Soon my windows were glazed over and the back of my camper frozen shut from the freezing rain.

As I lay dozing telling myself everything and everyone would be okay there was a crack so loud I thought lightning had struck a tree just yards away.

Seconds later I could hear the boys yelling, "Dad! Dad! The tarp's collapsed from all the ice."

Before I could get back out of my sleeping bag John was at the truck wearing just boots, hat, mittens, jacket and boxer shorts saying, "Stay there, Dad I'll fix it."

I couldn't sleep, there was too much racket from the ice hitting the roof and I was wondering if I had put my family into a precarious position.

I later figured at least 1 1/2 to 2 inches of ice had fallen within 10 minutes.

Soon the ice turned to snow and we were in a regular blizzard.

One of the boys hollered, "Dad it is snowing hard! Do you think we should get out of here?"

"No," I replied, "let's give it one hour and then decide."

Within a half-hour there must have been six inches of snow on top of the ice and there appeared to be no let up. With a sinking sensation in my heart I decided we had best get out and wondered if I had waited too long.

"Let's go boys. Pack it up," I hollered.

Getting dressed, I started the truck and let it idle. The comfortable rumble of the diesel helped calm my nerves.

Packing was a nightmare. The wind was blowing, snow was drifting everywhere and the ground was slippery from the ice. Luckily, the tarp had held on the other three corners and our packs, gear and tent were still protected. It was fairly quick work to get them into the truck

Trying to fold frozen tarps in a blizzard is something I would not wish on anyone. In fact we almost decided to leave them, when we were able to stuff them into the back of the truck.

Soon we were ready to go.

Questions started flying.

Which way did we come in? Can you see the road?

Slipping and sliding while in four-wheel-drive low range we started the long trip out.

Thank goodness we had scouted earlier, because the lay of the land and the road obscured by driving snow was still fresh in our memories.

Between the three of us we inched our way down the first hillside and started up another following faint lines in the snow we hoped were old tire tracks.

The diesel motor growled comfortingly, the tires spun, the cab was warm and for the first time that evening, I started to feel a little better about what we were doing.

It took awhile but eventually we were on the main road about eight miles above the town of Imnaha.

It was still snowing and we had a 15-percent downgrade ahead.

About a mile from Imnaha the snow turned to rain and I started to relax.

We made it to town with my hands hurting from clenching the wheel so tightly and parked in a churchyard where we spent the rest of the night.

It was several hours before daylight and once again after pulling out the tarps I climbed back into my warm comfortable sleeping bag.

Instead of re-pitching their tent John and Joe opted to sit and sleep in the cab. In the morning the mountains surrounding Imnaha were covered with snow.

"Well boys did you sleep well?" I asked as we stood huddled against the cold.

"Oh so-so," replied Joe. "How about you?"

"So-so" I replied.

"Tell you what," I said, "I'll buy breakfast in Joseph (37miles away) and we can decide on the way over what we are going to do."

On the way to Joseph we decided our bear hunting trip was over and our next option would be to explore the little towns that are always overlooked when storming down the road at 70 miles per hour.

Two days and many gunshops later, I pulled back into Coos Bay without a bear but with memories that will last me and my boys for the rest of our lives.

As I later related this story to family, friends, and acquaintances many questioned our wisdom of coming out of the woods in the middle of the night during a blizzard.

"Do you think you made a mistake?" they'd asked "after all it is spring and it wasn't going to snow forever."

"That's true," I answered, "but according to the local ranger it snowed off and on for the next six days and the road to Hat Point is now closed about three miles above Imnaha."

My answer now remains the same.

"No it wasn't a mistake; it was probably the smartest thing I have ever done. After all what father ever puts his sons at risk?"

BLUE MOON BUCK

Because I live in the midst of some of the best black-tail deer hunting country in Oregon, it is never necessary for me to camp and hunt. Within 15 minutes of leaving any restaurant in Coos Bay, I can be hunting.

For years my cronies and I ate at Dishners because they were open at 5, which is the time we usually met. That allowed for long, leisurely breakfasts and an opportunity to reminisce over past hunting exploits. It also allowed for planning to the enth degree, about what and where we were going to safely hunt after daybreak. When Dishners chose to open later in the day, we were forced to look elsewhere for our early morning breakfast.

What we found was the Blue Moon, which is best described as a friendly dive; a place where you could buy omelets, steaks, eggs, or just a roll all served by the 6-foot- 6, 300-pound cook/waiter, who, if you were not careful, would just as soon dump your order in your lap if you crossed or otherwise upset him.

It was in the Blue Moon where my hunting partners and I, over cold coffee, runny omelets and burned toast, (the huge cook/ waiter's specialty), decided where to hunt, thus the title.

We picked, Willanch a, spot about 20 minutes from the Blue Moon. Willanch, a valley made eons ago by the ocean, is now prime dairy land. It is the high country off the valley which we would hunt. The high country is filled with logged-over land called clear cuts.

Clear cuts become the bread baskets for deer and elk, which feed on the broad-leaf plants. Clear cuts remain prime hunting territory until new-growth fir trees reach heights of 8 feet or so when they start blanking out the broad leaf plants. The Willanch clear cut where we were headed was 2 years old and previous summer scouting trips showed it was full of deer.

Plans had been made at the Blue Moon as to who was hunting where. Ridges had been identified and assigned, and rallying points determined, as was who was to help whom in the event someone was successful.

Driving to a high point of land overlooking our hunt, as the hunt leader, I again pointed out who was to go where, with safety being the number-one issue on all of our minds.

My 16-year-old son, Joe; and his buddy, Ben Ferguson, would be off to my right. They had been instructed to move slowly down two different ridges pushing toward my brother- in-law, Jack, who would wait near the edge of the timber hoping to bag a buck which had been hiding in the clear cut.

My task was to side-hill across several other ridges while moving toward Jack in a big semi-circle. The idea was to trap any deer that might sneak out in front of Jack, while trying to avoid being seen by any of us.

The weather was cold and rainy as I slowly started into the hunt. Low-lying fog had settled into some of the hollows and draws, creating a beautiful scene of stark whites from the fog, and brilliant greens from the fir trees, all mixed with the broad leaf reds, golds and browns of fall, almost too pretty to describe.

Moving slowly, silently and carefully, I pushed from one ridge to the next, frequently stopping to glass, looking for elusive bucks. Within minutes, I spotted a doe with two fawns, standing stock still behind a vine maple. They were not watching me but my son, who was at least 500 yards away on another ridge. Smiling to myself, I watched as they slowly backed around the maple assuming they had never been seen.

By the time I reached my second ridge, a 300-yard uphill scramble, which left me huffing and puffing, I had spotted nine deer, all does and fawns. One of the fawns was a button buck, legal to shoot, but I was after bigger game.

As I reached the top of the next ridge, I removed my hat and collapsed to my knees, and haltingly knee-walked to a stump I hoped would allow me to glass the next open valley while staying hidden.

So much for the agony of walking on my knees over roughly logged ground. The first thing I saw was a big old doe looking me right in the eye. She tossed her head and flicked her tail as if to say, "You can fool some of the deer some of the time, and you can fool all the deer all of the time, but you cannot fool me. I've known where you were for the past 15 minutes," and bounded out of sight.

Resting behind my stump, I glassed for twenty minutes or more and saw nothing. I figured my runaway doe must have spooked the entire neighborhood when she ran off.

With that thought in my mind, I slowly got to my feet and looked around. Guess what? Further down the hill, about 200 yards away and out of sight from where I had been kneeling, was a white-nosed deer looking right at me. Grabbing my binoculars I looked and all I saw was horns, big horns. This was a buck worth writing home about.

Trembling slightly in eagerness and buck fever, I reached for my 14-inch 8MM JD Jones Contender tucked into a shoulder holster under my left arm. Slowly I dropped down behind another stump which I could use as a rest and looked for him in my 2 1/2 - 7 LER Burris scope.

He was gone.

Standing up, I figured if I moved about 15 feet to my right, I might get a chance for a shot if he headed for the timber on a trail we had found deer used, when scouting, in the summer. The only rest I could see in the area I wanted to move to, was a fire-blackened stump about 6 inches in diameter sticking about 2 feet above ground. I dropped down behind it, twisted my scope up to 5 power and waited.

Seconds, which seemed like hours passed, and no deer. "Where did he go?" I wondered. Suddenly, I saw movement. It was my deer, further away and moving fast, toward the sanctuary of the timber. Placing the crosshairs smack into the middle of the trail he was on, I waited for him to run into my sight picture. As soon as I saw his right front shoulder, I squeezed the trigger. Bang! He kept right on running and in less than a blink of the eye, he was gone, into the timber.

Mentally, I marked the spot where I last saw the buck, a broken-topped alder with one bent limb. Then I went back over the ridge and hollered to Jack, telling him I needed some help. I wanted Jack to sit on my shooting stump and guide me to the tree. This deer had been at least 250 yards away when I shot and it is very easy to get confused as to exact spots without someone helping.

As Jack guided me down to my tree, I picked up the deer's trail where I had first spotted him looking up at me. His tracks led me to the exact spot where I had fired and after telling Jack to come on down, I started casting about looking for signs of blood, or hair, a scuffed footprint anything which would indicate I had hit him.

I found nothing.

Tracking the deer into the woods proved almost futile. The ferns were soaking wet and waist high. Salal, Oregon grape and huckleberry bushes were intertwined into an almost impenetrable mass, making it almost impossible to move through. I started to feel a little sick. What if he were wounded? How was I going to find him?

Returning to the edge of the timber, I again picked up his tracks and slowly followed them into the brush. This time, by getting on my hands and knees, I was able to go another 15 yards or so before I lost the track. Still no sign of his being hit.

It was about this time Jack said, "I think I'll hunt down the next ridge. Maybe he went up on top. If I find his tracks, I will give you a yell."

Getting discouraged because I could not find any sign, I, too, was ready to quit. "Looks like I missed," I thought.

However, I could not quit. Something kept telling me the deer did not look quite right as he ran into the timber. I had also heard some faint crashing sounds from the top of the hill which could have been a deer thrashing about just before it died. Dad had instilled into me to always keep looking until I was sure I had missed. I was not sure, I had to keep looking.

Pushing through the bushes, casting about in an ever-larger circle, I still could not find any signs of blood or a wounded deer. By now, I was 80 or more yards into the timber, and more than 90 minutes had passed since I had shot. I was getting hot from my raingear, tired, and very discouraged and ready to quit a second time when I decided to sit down and rest.

After catching my breath for five minutes or so, I pushed myself upward and into a small clearing about 3feet across. Smack dab in the middle, was a huge dinner-plate-sized patch of bright red blood. "Yes! Yes!" I shouted. "Hey Jack! I have found blood."

Dead silence greeted my call.

Dropping a piece of toilet paper, to mark the spot, I again started to track my deer only this time, I was following a blood trail. Every time I found blood, I marked the spot with a bit of paper. This allowed me, by looking backward at the line of white paper, to see the direction in which the deer was traveling. It was not easy. I continually lost the trail and had to keep backing up.

Within 30 minutes or so, Jack arrived saying, "I figured you must have found something when you did not top the ridge." With him was my nephew, Dave Pappel, another handgun hunter, to help. Slowly, we moved another 25 or so yards into the timber until we lost the track all together.

Once again, I started casting in small circles around Jack who was standing on the last blood spot. It was on my third circle down next to the creek and about 15 feet from Jack when I spotted my buck. He was lying dead in the creek where he had fallen, after making one last giant leap.

My buck was a large 3-point. I want to say huge, but he wasn't. He just felt that way after we worked for several hours dragging him back to our truck. My son and his friend did most of the dragging. Those two husky, 16-year-olds dragged my buck uphill faster than I could walk. (It's tough getting old).

My bullet had entered the rib cage on the right side taking out both lungs, before exiting left. I used finding this buck as a teaching tool for my Joe and Ben. I pointed out that he had traveled more than 100 yards before dying. He never really showed he was hit before entering the timber and I, on two occasions, had wanted to quit looking because there were no signs. But the lessons taught me by my father were not forgotten.

In retrospect, it was one of the finest pistol shots I have ever made: one-shot kill at, at least 250 yards. However, if I had to do it all over again I think I might have let him go. Well, maybe I wouldn't. After all, I am a hunter.

A NEW
HAMPSHIRE MOOSE

It was the kind of morning in which your body makes your mind question why you hunt. My brother, Steve and I were in the predawn darkness of New Hampshire's opening day of moose season, walking down an old logging road being buffeted by wind and some rain. As the graying light of dawn brightened the trees around us the rain stopped, and I hoped that soon the sun would break through and warm our aching and aging bodies. We were tired, having scouted some hard miles over the past two days looking for a moose.

Moose hunting has always been a dream of mine. As a child growing up in New Hampshire, I always looked forward to the arrival of the L.L. Bean catalog and would spend hours huddled by our wood-burning stove looking and dreaming over the objects pictured for sale within its covers. One that stands out in my mind was an advertisement for an Old Town canoe showing a bewhiskered, red-checkered-jacket-wearing individual drifting down an unnamed river straight toward a huge bull moose.

Another moose memory revolves around an old calendar Dad had hanging in his gun room. The calendar was an advertisement for black powder manufactured by Laflin & Rand. The picture showed a hunter huddled under his overturned canoe reaching for a Model 95 Winchester as a huge bull moose peered at him from the brush. In my dreams, I knew someday I, too, would go moose hunting. Little did I know it would be more than 45 years before my dream came true.

Fifteen years before, the moose herd in New Hampshire had grown to the point that fish and wildlife authorities authorized a hunt for 50. Unfortunately for me, as a resident of Oregon, I learned too late about this new hunt and did not apply. However, I was ready the following year and submitted my application along with the required $10 and sat back with my fingers crossed, hoping I would be a successful applicant.

I wasn't.

For the next 13years, I faithfully applied for one of the 25 or so-out-of state tags and every year, around the 20th of June; I would call and ask one of my brothers, both residents of New Hampshire, if my name had been listed in the local newspaper as a successful applicant.

I would invariably hear, "No."

Even though hunting was allowed, the moose population continued to grow at an astounding rate. From the initial 50tags, New Hampshire's' Fish and Game department was soon letting 400-plus hunters pursue this wily creature.

Moose became so prevalent in the woods around our family camp in Pittsburg, we started calling them swamp donkeys for their long-legged, mud-throwing, rocking gait as they ran through the woods. Last fall, when I was hunting whitetail deer, I counted 22 different bulls over a two-day period.

When it comes to allocating hunting tags for moose, New Hampshire divides the state into 22different hunting zones. Individuals apply in descending order for the zones they want to hunt. Applicants also have the opportunity to restrict their applications by only applying for certain districts.

Those that are the most popular are found in the northern most part of the state, near the Canadian border, which just happens to be the area around the family camp, and the area I always picked as my first choice.

Because moose are so big, hunters are encouraged to take along a friend to help them if they are successful. These friends or partners are called subpermittees and they are allowed to carry firearms and hunt just like the permittee, the hunter who is issued the tag. But only one moose can be harvested between the two hunters.

Finally, after seven years my brother, Edward, was a successful applicant for the area around our family camp. He asked me to be his subpermittee and I declined, telling him I was too busy, even though I had applied for my own permit. Within a month of him successfully filling his tag with someone else as his subpermittees, he died, and I have always regretted telling him, no.

More years passed and I continued to apply, this time, telling my brother, Steve, I wanted him to be my subpermittee if I was successful.

Life moved on and every once in awhile for the next five months, I would occasionally dream of moose hunting and wonder, is this the year?

Around 9:30 a.m. on the third Friday in June, I happened to sit down at my computer and logged onto the fish and wildlife page in order to check on the status of the moose drawing. Why I picked that date or time I will never know unless it was my subconscious at work, because I had picked the exact date of the drawing and because of the three-hour time difference between Oregon and New Hampshire, the drawing had just been completed.

Quickly, I scanned the names of the successful applicants and once again my name was absent. So I clicked onto the list of alternates. An alternate list is maintained in the event one of the primary applicant declines a tag.

Yahoo! I couldn't believe it! There was my name, as alternate number 16. I was so excited I immediately called my brother to tell him I had been picked. Within minutes of hanging up the phone, it rang three more times as friends from New Hampshire called to tell me I was an alternate. It was then, the finding of my name on the alternate list, that I knew my dream of hunting moose was going to become to reality. Experience has shown the game authorities that alternates up to number 30 or so are usually awarded a moose tag and with me being 16 it was a given that sometime in the fall, I would be hunting moose.

Successful applicants are given until July 31 to pay their

appropriate fees and to confirm they will be hunting. Some decline and that is when the alternates are contacted. On August 7, I received an e-mail from the fish and wildlife department telling me I had been assigned wildlife management unit J1.

J1? I was heartbroken; I just assumed I would be given my first choice, A2 in Northern New Hampshire where I knew the country and could not get lost if I tried having hunted there for years. Reality set in and I decided J1 was better than no tag at all, but I had no idea what area it encompassed.

E-mail queries to and from the fish and wildlife people gave a rough outline of the area and I learned J1 is just minutes from my brother's house in Ashland, N.H. It included most of the land north of Squam Lake (Golden Pond), and Lake Winnipesaukee up to Conway. The western border was Highway 25 B and then east to the Maine/N.H. line. Further reading showed that the year before, 15 permits had been given for this area and 11 hunters were successful.

Maybe it wasn't so bad after all. So I sent in the money and then called Steve. However, my call was met with very little enthusiasm. His biggest complaint was we had never hunted that area and it would take a lot of scouting in order to be successful.

August 21 found my wife, Sue, and me, getting off the airplane at the Manchester airport. We had a busy schedule ahead of us. We planned to scout for moose, attend my 40th high school reunion, tour the Maritime Provinces and most importantly for me, to attend the three-hour moose class in Whitefield, required of all successful applicants.

The class is necessary so that everyone who hunts moose knows exactly what the law requires. Initially, I laughed when I first heard I had to attend the class in order to learn the basics of identifying, hunting, laws and regulations and caring for a downed moose. After all, I had seen hundreds in the North Country so I knew what they looked like. I have also killed many bull elk which are almost as large as a moose, or so I thought. I knew how to take care of large game. What could I learn or be taught?

It turned out to be a very interesting class albeit a little repetitive. Incidentally the portion of the moose class that reviews the laws and regulations is audio taped. All individuals are given exactly the same briefing by the same fish and wildlife police officer. Why? In the event you end up in court over a game violation, you cannot plead ignorance. Everyone has to sign in and out of the class as proof they attended before they are mailed their permits and tags. I learned this the hard way when I tried to leave early when the ending question-and-answer period disintegrated into a bull session.

I was politely turned back at the door and told if I did not stay till the bitter end I would not be issued my permit. After 14years of applying, I opted to stay.

For me, the most important aspect of the class was a review of the laws and regulations for hunting moose. For instance, only two individuals can be in the woods hunting from your party unless the third is a licensed guide. In Oregon, the more individuals one can entice into the woods while hunting, the more successful you will be, even though they are not armed. Another was a definition of roads, and the distance for you and the moose to be off the road before you can shoot: 300 feet.

Fifteen minutes after leaving my brother's house on our first scouting trip, we were looking at a bull moose. To add to our excitement, it was the first time Sue had ever seen a moose in the wild.

"All right!" I thought. "Moose hunting in J1 is going to be simple."

However, it was not to be.

During the August moose class, we were told moose would not be found in the swamps and bogs during hunting season. They would be in the high country usually near clear cuts where there is ample food.

Scouting two days before opening season on Steve and I returned to the spot where we had seen the moose hoping to see him or some fresh sign. We saw nothing, except old spoor and a few maple whips with their tops gnawed off.

We did not get too excited about the lack of sign, but as the day wore on, and we covered a lot of ground, we became more discouraged, because we did not see anything that shouted, "moose!"

The next day, Friday, we moved even farther away, following

the advice of some local hunters. Still no sign and the pressure was building. Opening day was in less than 24 hours and after having walked 10 or 15 miles a day, I was thinking we might never see a moose.

Late that afternoon we returned, to the same spot where we had seen the moose in August. Our intent was to go clear to the top of the mountain to see if he was up there hiding out. He wasn't.

As we were starting to drive off just at dark, to head for home and a cup of hot tea another pickup came into view. I could see they were hunters because there was a shotgun hanging in the rear window and the passenger was dressed in a red and black-checkered jacket usually worn for fall hunting.

Rolling down my window, I stuck out my head and hollered, "Where are the moose?"

Surprised, the passenger looked startled and then he smiled and said, "Out in the woods."

"No they aren't," I replied. "We have been looking for them for two days and have not seen one or any fresh sign."

Slowly the conversation warmed. After asking us our names, the passenger told us he had known our dad when he had worked in a neighboring town as police chief. Pretty soon, we were playing the, do-you-know-who game, and our world soon became smaller. The driver lived two streets away from my sister in Lakeport, and his kids had played with her kids, when they were young and all had attended school together.

Before we parted, we were told to call a Mrs. Connelly who lived in Sandwich about a 30-minute drive from my brother's house, and ask her permission to hunt on her posted land. The driver told us to use his name, as he was sure permission would be granted. He also said he thought there was a clear cut high on the mountain above Mrs. Connelly's place and we might find a moose or two.

Mrs. Connelly was contacted and she graciously consented to allow us to hunt. She told us the property was posted because she wanted to keep track of who was there. When I told her we would park out on the road by her house so as to not wake her in the early morning she said, "No, please park by the barn. That way I know you are here and your truck will be safe."

The following morning found Steve and me at Mrs. Connelly's 240-acre farm and woodlot. It was dark, cold and wet as we slowly followed an old logging road up into the woods. I was carrying an Encore rifle in 338 Winchester and Steve, his favorite 14-pound, single-shot, an 8 Bore Thomas Bland loaded with 11 drams of black powder and a 1200 grain soft lead bullet.

The idea was if we saw a moose up close and not moving too fast, one of us-preferably me, would shoot it with this antique rifle. However, hunting conditions would have to be perfect before either one of us tried.

By 8 o'clock, we were high up on the side of the mountain. We were moving in a crescent shape headed north and west, all the while looking for fresh sign and the clear cut that was supposed to be near the top.

Around 9, the woods to the north started to clear and we knew that the elusive clear cut was close by. It was surprising how close to the top it was. We had almost given up on ever finding it and had just agreed we might as well go to the lookout and enjoy the view, if the weather allowed overlooking Lake Winnipesaukee,. Discovering the clear cut eliminated that plan.

Separating and occasionally drawing on our home-made moose call a coffee can with some rawhide hanging out the bottom. We looked over the clear cut for moose that might be out feeding. No such luck, but the clear cut was bisected by many ridges and it was necessary to go over them to see clear to the backside of the opening.

When we reached the midpoint, we found the first fresh moose sign we had seen in two and a half days: moose crap, hoof prints, and freshly nibbled maple tops. The moose crap was bright and shiny, and almost warm to the touch. We knew moose were close by; all we had to do was find them.

If you picture the clear cut as a long, narrow kitchen table, it wasn't until we were in the lower left corner headed for the timber that I found some tracks which appeared to be going into and out of the clear cut.

Steve is the better tracker, so I called him over and showed him what I had discovered.

With a big grin on his face he whispered, "Moose."

"Which way?" I asked.

"Down into the hemlocks. Looks like there might be two or three. Let's follow the tracks and see what we can find."

Slowly we set out. Steve was tracking and I was off to his right about 15 feet or so and just a little in front of him, looking everywhere trying to see a moose watching his back trail before he saw me.

Fifteen minutes or so after we started into the timber, we heard a loud crack off to our left. Instantly I crouched, flipped off my scope covers and scanned under the trees trying to see what it was we had spooked.

We both hoped it was moose, but where were they?

Frantically, Steve waved me back up toward him, whispering, "Moose! Moose! I see them."

Turning, I saw a big old cow and another moose, about 70 yards away peering myopically around a hemlock tree.

Taking aim, I saw her turn and start to run uphill. Right behind her was the biggest bull moose I had seen and he, too, was moving fast. Aiming between two trees I knew he was going to pass between, I waited until I had a clear shot at his body and pulled the trigger. Ka whomp! My bull was hit and hit hard; he immediately turned and started following the contour of the land. Reloading and taking aim because I did not want him to get away, I fired again.

There is a cow! There is a cow!" I heard Steve whisper. "Don't shoot the cow."

Even though it was legal to shoot a cow, because I had an any sex tag, we were after a bull and until I fired the second time, he thought I was shooting at the cow.

It wasn't till after the excitement died down that we realized I had hit a rock instead of the bull with my second shot. When I fired, I saw what I thought was a huge water spray similar to those that occur when one shoots an elk in the pouring rain. The spray however was a small rock that somehow got between me and the moose.

My second shot put the moose into high gear, running straight away. I had the shakes so badly my scope was wobbling all over. Taking a deep breath and chastising myself for having moose fever, I again took careful aim right where his neck meets his shoulders and touched off other round.

This time he dropped, dying.

I was shaking so badly I had to sit down to catch my breath. As Steve congratulated me and shook my hand, the realization sunk in that I had just killed a bull moose. A lifetime dream had just been fulfilled.

Slowly we approached, and the closer we got, the larger his antlers and body became until I was almost overwhelmed by the size and the enormity of what I (we) had done. His size made our elk look small.

We were more than two miles from the truck and at our feet lay the largest animal I have ever killed. "Now what?" kept running through my mind.

We retraced out steps, reviewing exactly where we were when we heard the first crack, to the final shot. We determined there were actually three moose, the cow and bull, which had run uphill; and another, sex unknown, which went down.

We took pictures, congratulated one another and discussed our hunt, how everything had worked out so perfectly, putting off the inevitable gutting chore.

The ground was so steep it was possible for us to wrestle him around for better gutting position. Soon I was shoulder deep into entrails and before long, the job was done and we were deciding how far we could move him.

The steep ground was an asset. Over the next two hours we were able to drag this huge animal down hill about 300 yards. There were times we had to get out of the way as his massive weight propelled him down on his own and threatened to over run us.

Finally, tree tops and downed branches wouldn't allow us to go any farther. Seven years before New Hampshire had one of its worst ice storms in recorded history. Literally millions of trees were toppled or destroyed when the weight of the ice coupled with a strong wind caused them to drop like bowling pins. Now those broken treetops had us stopped cold.

So we separated. I stayed behind, while Steve went for the backpacks we had left in the truck, his chainsaw and, hopefully, some helping hands.

Shortly after leaving, he came upon an old grown-over logging road that ran straight to the house of Mrs. Connelly, which saved him a considerable amount of time hiking back to his truck.

Calling from Mrs. Connelly's, he discovered no one was home at his place or at his son, Jamie's. There was just one last chance for some help; so he called his friend, Randy.

Fortunately for us, Randy was home.

It is traditional for Randy, Steve and their friends to gather at the garage on Saturday afternoons to drink a few beers and swap hunting and snow machine stories.

Reaching Randy, Steve told him where he was, that we had a moose down, and that we needed help including chainsaws and ropes.

Back on the mountain I was cold and chilled. I had worked up a sweat dragging the moose down the mountain and it was starting to rain and blow. I walked up and down to get warm; I had forgotten matches so I could not build a fire and my jacket wasn't really appropriate unless I was moving for a New Hampshire windy and rainy afternoon.

What was really hard for me was I did not have anything to read. I am not one of those who are content to sit and vegetate and time passed so slowly. I had nothing to occupy my mind, except to replay the hunt over and over.

Two and half hours after Steve left, I thought I heard a chainsaw way off in the distance down where he had earlier disappeared. However, the wind was blowing so hard I couldn't really tell.

Minutes later I thought "That is two chainsaws, maybe three or more. I wonder if it's Steve?"

Soon, the air was alive with the sound of saws and falling trees. Draping my moose antlers with my blaze orange hunting vest to make him easier to find, I followed the sound down the mountain to see what was going on.

It wasn't two or three chainsaws it was five. Randy had shown up with three men, Ronny Currier, Danny Currier, Joe Cadorette, all skilled in the use of chainsaws. I was so happy to see so many guys willing to help me, I almost wept.

Mrs. Connelly had given Steve permission to clear the old logging road he had found on his way out, something she had wanted to get done for two years. In a matter of hours they cut two miles of road up the mountainside to within 900 yards of where my moose lay.

Leaving three saws with the truck, we all went into the brush headed back to the moose. After recovering him we tied a huge rope around his antlers and two guys with saws started cutting a path through the dead falls back toward the truck. The rest of us cleared the trail and dragged the moose.

About the time I thought I would drop from exhaustion, I saw the truck's tail lights and knew the back-breaking work was almost done. With one last pull and a huge burst of adrenaline, we pulled like crazy and had our moose up to the back of the truck.

Utilizing the truck's dump bed, a block and tackle and seven guys pulling, we soon had the moose loaded. Exhausted we all headed down out of the woods to Mrs. Connelly's.

I have never seen a landowner so excited about someone bagging an animal on their property as she was. Even though it was cold, dark and rainy, she stood around the truck admiring "her" moose for approximately 15 minutes, all the while regaling us with tales of the family Norwegian elk hounds, transient moose and hunting with her husband years before.

We arrived back in Ashland at Steve's house, too late to make the 5 o'clock closing of the fish and wildlife checking station. New Hampshire Fish and Wildlife officials require all hunter-tagged moose be weighed, a tooth extracted in order to determine age and location of kill, before they are again tagged by them for transport to a butcher.

So that task would have to be completed in the morning.

As a lifelong hunter I have learned the tastiest wild game is that which is cooled as quickly as possible. Our moose had been dead for more than eight hours and its hide was still on, holding in tremendous amounts of heat that could lead to meat spoilage. I was in a hurry to get it skinned.

Removing the moose from the back of Steve's truck was done

with his backhoe. A gambrel was inserted into the moose's hind legs and then chained to the front bucket and gently lifted into the air.

Lowering the animal to the ground allowed us to start skinning the hindquarters and as we progressed toward the head, the bucket was lifted, enabling us to get the hide off rather quickly. As we skinned, plumes of condensation arose from the animal's still-warm body as heat met the cold air.

At one point, it seemed as if half the towns of Ashland and Holderness had come to help or watch us work. Every time I looked up from skinning, there were new faces gathered around. The one common denominator was they all grinned in approval.

The next morning, Sunday, we again loaded our skinned and well-cooled moose back into the truck for the trip to the New Hampton, checking station. There, we learned our moose was 6 ½ years old, and was carrying antlers that measured 54 inches at their widest point. Best of all, it weighed 804 pounds dressed out, which meant my siblings, would have meat for the winter.

Returning home and reflecting on my successful hunt I am just realizing it was the hunt of a life time and the fulfillment of a dream first realized many, many years ago.

WITH ONE GOOD SHOT,
A NEWCOMER BAGS HIS BUCK

The September 28th, 1996 opening day of deer season in Coos Bay was unusual in many respects. The first was the date, it was a week early. Another was for the first time in many years neither of my sons, John or Joe, would be hunting with me. John because he is in his first full time job after graduating from college and had work commitments. Joe was in his first full week at Oregon State University (pledge week) and could not make it home.

The early morning fog, after a week of bluebird weather, was so thick we could not start hunting until 11:00 a.m., which was about the time the sun burned it away. Interestingly enough our hunting party of six sat in my old suburban telling hunting stories from 6:00 to 11:00 am and we never repeated a story.

One of those listening was a young man; a friend of Joe's named Grady Bourell. Grady's Dad works on tug boat for Sause Brothers, a local shipping company. His tug is on a long slow return trip from Japan. Knowing I would have wanted him to take my son's hunting if the situation was reversed, I invited Grady to accompany our hunting party.

Grady has hunted some, what is more important he is safety conscious and an excellent rifle shot. Because of his experience I added a few caveats to the invitation. The first and most important were as a newcomer he was to do exactly as I told him or he would never be invited to hunt with us again.

We as a group of hunters are extremely conscious of safety. Most of us have hunted together for years and know what we are supposed to do to insure our safety. The only newcomers taken into our group have been our sons (unfortunately there are no daughters to teach). No one joins or goes hunting with us until they have the permission of everyone involved.

As the quasi leader of this nefarious group, I usually am the one who proposes new members such as Ben Ferguson whom I introduced several years ago. Ben's Dad is not a hunter but he expressed, through Joe, an interest in hunting and I have to admit he was an excellent candidate.

There is also a selfish reason. At 51, I am no longer spry, agile or able to run down an elk herd like I used to 25 years ago. Our group needs strong legs and arms, powerful lungs, and a willingness to help the old guys get their game out of the woods.

Grady is 18 and meets this description.

What would you have done with someone who wanted to hunt, and his Dad at sea? One other caveat for Grady was to observe and listen and ask questions and be prepared to explain our hunting plan to anyone anytime. The theory being if he said something incorrectly it could be corrected before the actual hunt.

Remember my opening paragraph about an opening day full of unusual experiences?

Well, another was our place to eat, The Mill Casino decided 5:00 am was too early to open and changed its hours to 6:00 am. Of course the casino is open 24 hours a day but not its restaurant. Readers will remember we started going there last year when they offered a $2.00 breakfast.

You can imagine the consternation that developed when we showed up to eat and were told, "You'll have to eat in the snack bar."

Of course the snack bar consists of a long counter with eight or so bar stools and three small two-man tables sandwiched between the bar and serving counter.

Not a good place to sit, eat and plan but we shoved the tables together and things worked out.

Heading out to the planned hunt area, the swish, swish of my wipers told me and the rest of the crew that the early morning coastal fog was going to be thick. Thick fog usually holds tight and keeps us from hunting until it is burned off by the rising sun.

Experience had taught most of us that it could be anywhere from nine am till noon. Sometimes it is possible to drive above it, and we decided, while still in the truck, to head up and see if we could get above the fog.

We couldn't and decided to sit awhile, drinking coffee, tea, pop while talking.

The conversations started with who was carrying what and why. Most of us have a half dozen or more Contenders to choose from and a different reasons for carrying them.

For instance I was packing my 14 inch Bullberry in 28-30 Stevens. I was going to carry my new TCA 10th anniversary .223 but lost my nerve. It is too nice to scuff. Well at least this week I thought it was.

Tracker Dave had his 14 inch .309 JD Jones, Ben his 300 Savage, Grandpa a BAR in 30-06 and Grady with my 14 inch .309 JD Jones and Rick his .308 Model 99 Savage.

Tracker Dave would not be caught dead hunting in the woods without his .309 JD Jones. His hunting prowess with the .309 was detailed in previous issues of **One Good Shot**. Do you remember my story of the huge bear he killed last year?

Grandpa has carried his 30-06 BAR as long as I have hunted with him. I married his daughter in 1969 so it's been a year or two.

Ben is still waffling as to what particular cartridge he prefers in the Contender. He started with a Model 99 .300 Savage and graduated to .300 Savage Bullberry barrel last year. Occasionally he will mutter about buying a .309 or 8mm JD Jones. I think he is waiting for the Encore in .308. However, as a college student, his funds are limited and I think he will wait a year or two.

Rick has carried his father's Model 99 in .308 for so many years he would not dream of using a handgun.

Grady as you know is the new hunter in our group. Grady is the neighbor's son who grew up with my son Joe. His family of rifle hunters understands and appreciates the challenges of handgun hunting. They were just a little slow making the change.

Over the past 12 or so years Grady watched my sons and I bag deer and elk with our Contenders and this year he wanted to try. Fortunate enough to have several Contenders to pick from, I lent him the .309 he was carrying.

Conversation in the truck quickly developed into a marathon of, "Do you   remember when I shot, and you shot, such and such a deer?"

As we sat and talked the fog got heavier, the windshield began to run with water and I turned the key to clear the glass.

By 9 am, I could not stand the inaction any longer. Getting out of my truck I told the rest of the crew, except for Grandpa who was snoozing in the corner, "I am going for a walk, maybe I'll catch a big buck, a mile or two, down the road."

"Wait, wait I'll go with you," came repeated cries from the interior of my truck.

Regrouping, I separated everyone into two groups, one bunch to head west, the other east down the cat road for 30 minutes. After which time we would regroup at the truck.

For the next hour all we did was walk in the fog. If we had not been on a cat road we all would have been lost in minutes. The fog was so thick it blurred my binoculars as I tried to peer ahead. It whitened my eyebrows and rain ran off the end of my nose.

Returning to the truck for more coffee, tea and hot chocolate we discussed what we had seen, if anything in the fog hunt.

Interestingly enough each group had spotted a forked horn buck. Forked horns are legal but because this was opening morning, no one wanted to fill their tag so early. If you are wondering how could they see them when all I have written about is the fog, it's because they were close. Visibility for most of the morning ranged from 20 to 50 feet.

It was not long before we were again reminiscing about the hunting days of yesteryear. It always amazes me how many times I can hear a particular story and how entranced I am to hear it all again.

By 10:30 the sky had brightened and we knew it would not be very long before we could hunt.

At 10:45 I could not stand it anymore. I quietly slid out of the truck saying, "Let's go Dave, I think we need to get into position, the rest of you guys; take off."

Grady, Rick, and Ben, with Grandpa driving, headed back down the gravel road to be dropped off at their pre-assigned ridges. What we do is encircle a clear cut and slowly push through, hoping to drive out deer. This hunt had been planned to push towards Grandpa and Grady.

It took me 15 or so minutes for me to walk to my pre-assigned ridge. By the time I got into position high on top of the ridge, I could see the sun shining through the fog. Everything below was still enveloped in a huge, white, rippling fluffy blanket.

Tucking up against a huge old fire blackened fir stump I waited for the sun to burn it away.

While half dozing in the warmth of the sunshine, I realized I could see Ben on his ridge top about 400 yards away.

Resting my Contender on top of the stump, I grabbed my hat and waved it as a signal to Ben that I was about to "side-hill" over towards the next ridge. We had already discussed when a hunter moves, someone else needs to sit and glass, hoping to see deer moving out in front of the hunter.

Our type of hunting includes signals that we have perfected which allow us to silently communicate vast distances without alerting deer.

Some of our signals are probably used by other hunters, but the main idea is for us to occasionally glass one another in case messages need to be shared.

For instance, a pat on the bottom means I am going to sit down and I want you to get up and push. Patting the top of your head indicates you can see deer on your partner's ridge but they are does. Hands and arms held over the head, fingers spread widely indicate you have seen a buck, the higher the hands are held, the bigger the buck. Arms held straight out from your sides with palms up means "where in heck are they?" Walking your fingers across the palm of your hand means both the observer and observee need to slowly walk towards one another. There are others, but I think you get the picture.

After a slow and arduous walk of 100 yards (side-hilling is really difficult) or so, I plopped down behind another stump.

Checking my Contender to insure it was safe, I picked up my binoculars to check out the far hillside for deer.

While glassing I picked out the rest of my hunting party and decided I would slowly walk down the ridge towards another stump that I thought would give me a better view of our hunting bowl.

As the sun rose higher and the day warmed, I found myself shedding my coat as we all slowly moved towards the far end of the bowl where Grandpa was sitting. The fog was long gone and this late in the morning the only sign of deer was beds and tracks made earlier under cover of the night and fog.

Picking up an old elk trail, I started following it from ridge to ridge. Because side-hilling is tough work, any chance to find an easier way is taken.

Deer and elk, in fact all game, always know the easiest way to travel while maintaining their elevation.

Signaling that I was going to sit and glass in front of Ben, I sat down behind a stump, (they make perfect rests for handgun hunters,) and placed my loaded Contender and a few extra shells out in front of me and started glassing.

Grady mistook my signal and got up to move. Luckily he saw my signal to sit back down and watch the ridge out to my left.

Ben had only moved a few hundred feet when I heard a click, click off to my right. Turning I saw two big bucks, who with one bound went out of sight .

They were out of my sight but headed straight towards Tracker Dave. Silently standing and waiting for Dave to shoot I heard a shot off to my right, and a voice calmly say, "I got one."

"Wow," I thought, "that was Grady; He must be at least 300 yards away."

"Nah, impossible, it could not have been him shooting, he's too far away." "Well maybe he did shoot but at what?"

Throwing caution to the winds, I stood up and hollered, "Grady what did you get?"

He replied, "I shot one of the two bucks that went under Dave. It rolled down the hill into the brush and now I can't see it."

"Stay there," I replied. "I'll go out to where you last saw it and track it down for you."

One of the problems hunters new to this country have is after shooting a deer they think they can walk right over to the spot where the animal was killed. They usually cannot if the deer was any distance away because the country looks so different up close than it did two or three hundred yards away. Experience has taught us to let the shooter sit tight and have someone else find the game and that is what I set out to do.

However, by the time I had cleared several ridges, Rick and Tracker Dave were already at the scene admiring Grady's excellent four point buck.

That was the day Grady became an accepted member of our hunting party. We decided anyone, who can bag a four point buck while hunting with a Contender, for the first time at better than 250 yards with one shot, is welcome.

A DIFFERENT KIND OF
ONE GOOD SHOT

I have hunted for years, ever since I was old enough to tag along after my father, as we hunted deer, rabbits and partridges in the woods of New Hampshire.

Today, my sons tag along after me, as we hunt elk, bear and deer in Western Oregon. What I want you to do is tag along with us as we go on one of our hunting trips.

John, Joe and I, left the house early one morning to glass a huge clear cut which we knew was home to a herd of Roosevelt elk. While glassing we spotted a huge bull elk about three-quarters of a mile away standing tall and majestically as he guarded his harem. Even at that distance, we knew we were looking at a big one and we were going to get him.

Excitedly, we planned our attack, determining who was going to go where and who was going to do what. We were all filled with that undefinable feeling that only occurs when you know the chase is on.

Slowly, we began our stalk. We were lucky. The elk were feeding away from us and there was no wind.

We decided to split up in order to cut down on noise and agreed to meet by a huge snag on the edge of the clear cut we had earlier identified.

Slowly and silently, I moved my mind racing and thoughts roaring, "This is it! This is the big one! This is a TROPHY, and this is a record book TROPHY!"

I could hardly wait to hang him on our wall.

Telling myself to creep, and go slowly, I listened carefully, hoping I would not hear my sons as they continued their own personal stalks. I knew if I were quiet, and they were quiet, HE would be there when we arrived.

Other thoughts raced through my mind as I slowly moved upward.

I wondered if ancient Native Americans had felt as I was feeling. Perhaps they had hunted this same place, this same trail. For some unexplained reason, I felt closeness to them and to other hunters, who had gone before me. I felt as though they were present, coaching and encouraging me to go slowly, pointing out a twigs to be stepped over, and trees to crouch behind.

It seemed to take forever, but in about an hour, I reached the snag to discover my younger and more fleetfooted sons had gotten there first.

"Geeze Dad!" whispered John, "you sounded like a steam locomotive huffing and puffing your way up the hill; I'm surprised you didn't scare our bull."

Too pooped to respond, I gestured silently, pointing to a log half-way into   the clear cut. This log would be close enough for a good shot and also afford an excellent rest for steadying our weapons.

Slowly, we started crawling, and once again, my mind started racing, thinking of the differences between these early hunters and what we were doing.   The early hunters hunted for food and survival, while we hunt for pleasure, sport, excitement and food.

We had to crawl on wet muddy ground for the last 50 yards, even through fresh elk droppings, but we did not care, we were after our trophy.

Our trophy would be a head that we could hang with pride in our living room.

Hung so all who entered would have to stop and ask, "Who got him?

We finally reached the log, and slowly, ever so slowly, raised our heads. There he was, less than 50 yards away and still unaware of our presence.

I silently positioned our weapon over the log, sighted carefully and slowly squeezed the trigger. There was no bang, just a gentle click, as my camera recorded him forever.

We had gotten our trophy.

Carefully, I squeezed the button several more times before the mighty bull became aware of our presence. Snorting loudly, alerting his harem to danger he wheeled and trotted off to the timber to become someone else's trophy on another day.

OCHOCO ANTELOPE

I had the good fortune to draw an antelope tag for the Ochoco Unit. There were 130 tags issued with published odds of 12 percent of getting one. With these odds, I was truly excited when the coveted tag arrived in July.

The Ochocos are a group of mountains located in Central Oregon. Oregon's rifle / handgun antelope season is always in August, usually for six days and starts around the 14th. Oregon's antelope herd is small, and bagging one of these elusive creatures is considered to be a real hunting feat. In fact, the herd is so small, when you receive a tag you are automatically put on a computer list that prevents you from applying or receiving another tag for five years. I have known hunters who have waited 12, 15, even 20 years to go antelope hunting in Oregon.

Upon receiving my tag, I mentally debated as to what Contender I was going to use, finally settling on the 6.5 JD Jones. Its trajectory and speed were, I figured, more than adequate for any hunting I intended to do.

In late July, my hunting partner, Orvel Bird, and I headed east for some preliminary scouting. Neither had ever hunted antelope, nor had we hunted in the Ochocos, so we were on a scouting trip, looking for appropriate areas to camp, hunt, and enjoy the great outdoors. Eight hard hours of driving brought us to the town of Mitchell, where we camped for the night. We spent the next two days looking for antelope, and a place to hunt. Everywhere we went, we saw, no-hunting or no-trespassing signs, even one that read: "NO HUNTING OR TRESPASSING, SURVIVORS WILL BE SHOT AGAIN."

There were lots of antelope. We sat and glassed for hours but they were always behind these anonymous and forbidding signs. Attempts to talk to the landowners proved futile. Most of the ranches were under the care of managers who said they did not have the authority to grant hunting privileges, or that the ranch was leased by a hunting club. One manager was willing to let us hunt if we would pay a $500 trespass fee, but we opted not to pay.

We became very discouraged. We wanted to hunt antelope, but were not willing (read that as rich enough) to pay the trespass fee, so Orvel and I went looking for help.

The best advice we received was from an Oregon Fish and Wildlife trooper. He told us to go back to Bend and get a BLM (Bureau of Land Management) lease map. These maps show just what acreage the ranches are leasing for grazing rights. The trooper said, "Ranchers routinely post all of the land, even if they are only leasing portions in order to prevent trespassers. However, they have no legal right to prevent hunting on government land if they do not lease it."

The BLM lease map proved to be a blessing. One of the biggest ranches, the one with the most obnoxious signs and with the most antelope, only leased a small portion of the area they had posted. Orvel and I knew where we were going to hunt.

On the long drive back to Coos Bay, I reluctantly decided not to use a handgun, but opted to use another Contender instead. The TCR 83 in 7MM Remington Magnum. Why you might ask? I knew my 6.5 JD Jones was more than adequate for antelope at any distance. However, the entire time we were scouting, Orvel and I never got within 400 yards of an antelope. I know there are those hunters including me, who have shot their Contenders at distances exceeding 400 yards, but I wanted the added stability a rifle provides for my first antelope.

Returning in August, we set up camp in a grove of willows beside a small creek. Just beyond the willows was a fence with no-hunting and no-trespassing signs posted every 100 yards or so.

Inside the fence was a huge sage brush-covered flat about 600 acres or more, filled with gullies, draws and most importantly, a herd of antelope with three large bucks. Our lease map showed that the property immediately in front of our camp was government land. In fact, the entire flat except for the far corner was not leased, but it was posted. That night, as I went to sleep listening to coyotes howl, and watching stars so brilliant they appeared to be just inches above my nose, I just knew I was going to be a lucky hunter.

Opening day found us up way before dawn. The air was crisp and cold because there had been a slight frost. I shivered and shook as I got dressed and then started the Coleman stove, boiling water and frying bacon. It seemed like hours passed before the water boiled and I could wrap my hands around a huge mug of sweetened steaming tea. My shivering and shaking stopped as I sipped the hot tea, flipped bacon and dreamed of the antelope I was going to get that day.

Shortly before dawn I slipped under the barbed-wire fence, just under the sign that read, "Trespassers will be shot, survivors will be shot again," and low-crawled to a gully I knew would take me far out into the flat without being detected by the wary antelope. The morning passed quickly. The herd with three nice bucks stayed hundreds of yards away. Around noon, the temperature rose into the low 80s, making it difficult to see as heat waves distorted anything out beyond 300 yards. Returning to camp, I was encouraged to see that the herd I had been watching was feeding in our direction. Maybe, just maybe, they would get close enough for me to take a shot.

Orvel and I decided to take a nap, with the idea of sneaking back out into the flat as the afternoon cooled. Awakening around 3, I sat and glassed the flat while hidden behind some sage brush. The bucks I had watched earlier had fed into our direction and appeared to be no more than 500 or 600 hundred yards away. I decided I would just sit and wait and see how close they would get. Deciding that the best thing to do was to stay quiet and let them feed right into camp proved to be a mistake, as some ranch hands came roaring across the flat in a pickup, no doubt attempting to get a shot, but all they did was scatter the herd, including the three bucks.

Around 7 o'clock, I started my low crawl back out into the flat as the herd started to regroup. I was hoping I could pick off a buck as he made his way back to the herd.

I don't know where he had been hiding or where he had come from, but on one of my sweeps with the glasses I saw a buck antelope feeding off to my right front. He appeared to be about 400 yards away, and I knew he was going to be mine. Resting my TCR 83 across my hat which I had placed on a small sage bush for a very steady rest, I took slow careful aim and fired and missed. He never even picked up his head.

How could I have missed? As an antelope feeds, it is constantly stopping to look around always aware of everything within its incredible eyesight range. I decided to low crawl closer moving when his head was down stopping when he looked around. Unfortunately for me he was feeding away as fast as I crawled. After 20 minutes, I was not any closer than I had been when hiding in the gully. It was going to be dark soon, so I decided I would take another shot.

This time I took into account the wind which was blowing from right to left and the fact that he was a heck of a lot further away than I thought. Holding real high and left to allow for distance and wind drift, I again took slow careful aim and pulled the trigger. He disappeared at my shot. Rising to my feet, ever wary of those, "trespassers will be shot again" signs, I headed out for where I hoped my antelope lay. I made 623 steps before I found him. Deciding not to field dress him on the spot proved easy, because I could see headlights coming from the direction of the ranch. No doubt it was the watchman coming to find out who was shooting on his ranch.

Orvel and I starting dragging and it soon became apparent that it was going to be a race as to who was going to get to camp first, us or the fast approaching pickup. We won. Just as I pulled my antelope under the wire and into camp an old battered truck pulled up and stopped. The driver with a friendly grin said, "Well, nice buck. Where did you get him?"

With my head and chin, I pointed off down the way he had come and said, "You know the old draw you just crossed, down there, just this side of the wire."

The old driver just sat and grinned and then said, "Well, good shooting, son. That was a damn fine long shot. You'll be amazed at how many of our bucks die on this side of the wire."

"Saying Good Night," he drove off.

SHEEPSHEAD TRIO

For years my hunting partners and I hunted blacktail deer in the Oregon coast foothills. For the same amount of time we always talked about hunting mule deer in eastern Oregon but job commitments and prime blacktail hunting keep us from venturing to the east.

However, the rapid rise in the cougar population which Oregonians were no longer allowed to hunt using dogs and the ban on logging to protect the spotted owl and marbled murrelet meant the rapid decline of the deer population.

Why?

A cougar will kill a deer a week for food but are known to kill others for the sheer sake of killing. Protecting birds, meant the end of clearcuts, (which I call Mother Nature's bread baskets) where the type of forage necessary to sustain deer herds would grow. In other words deer cannot survive by eating full grown fir trees and their population declined over sixty percent in the past ten years.

My hunting partners and I retired from the everyday workforce and were able to take the time to apply for and get tags to pursue mule deer. Initially we were not very successful as hunters. The terrain of sage brush and mahogany coupled with long range shooting was so different it took us several years to make the change from black tail to mule deer hunters.

This past fall was different. Before the season was over nine tags out of ten were filled which by anyone's indicators meant we were learning the best way to hunt this markedly different terrain.

Several bucks were killed on opening weekend. However, the full moon followed by hot sunny days meant deer were feeding at night and then sticking tightly to their shaded beds during the day. About the only way to see one was to jump them out by pushing the sage, timber, greasewood or mahogany flats.

Monday turned out to be another hot day and by eight a.m. sweat was coursing down my back and running off my forehead as I climbed a steep ridge coming off Sheepshead Mountain.

Stopping to take a swallow or two from my water bottle, one of my hunter partners who was on the top of Sheepshead called on his hand held radio to tell me he had spotted a forked horn buck and doe moving into a draw about 250 yards to his front.

This meant that they should be about five hundred yards to my front and slightly to my right. Moving carefully and very slowly because it was hot and steep, I continued making my way to the top, always alert knowing the deer spotted earlier might jump and run when I got close.

Crossing from one side to the other as I slowly climbed, I made sure to glass the draws on each side of the ridge. Peering intently into the shadows looking for the leg, back, horn, ear or nose that a mule deer might think was hidden.

Timing my crossing pattern to hit the area and draw when my partner said he had seen deer, I was startled when not one, not two, but three bucks exploded out of the grease wood growing in the draw and headed for the top running as only spooked deer can run.

Dropping to a sitting position, I placed the crosshairs of my single shot Encore in 7 mm Remington Magnum several feet out in front of the biggest buck and pulled the trigger.

Down he went rolling, struggling to get to his feet.

Quickly reloading with my heart running like a trip hammer and mouth dry as a cotton ball, I took a lead on the second buck fired and missed. Frantically, I reloaded just in time to see the first buck struggle to his feet. Again I fired at him and down he went.

Reloading I went back to the second buck which was hightailing it for safety. Again I lead him but a little further this time, fired and down he went dropping as though he had been hit over the head with a hammer.

The last buck was now running full tilt and about 175 yards away. Swinging my crosshairs along side his body, just as though I was goose hunting, I passed his chest area and pulled the trigger when I thought my lead was sufficient enough to dump him.

Again I missed or so I thought.

Fortunately for me he slowed way down and looked back probably trying to figure out where his buddies had gone. Taking another bead on my now walking deer I pulled the trigger and he dropped as though running full into a concrete wall.

As I mentally marked all the areas where I had deer down the hand held radios went nuts.

"Who's shooting?"

"Shoot'em before he gets away!"

"Whatever happened to one good shot?"

"Did you get him?"

Picking up my radio, I calmly said, "Sometimes you have to shoot more than once if there is a whole flock of them."

Again voices poured out of the speaker.

"What?"

"You mean you got more than one?"

"You are kidding right; no one can shoot and reload a single shot that fast?"

"I heard six shots does that mean six deer?"

Within a few minutes one of my hunting partners appeared and I directed him to the area where the first buck, a beautiful balanced four point had disappeared. He was still alive when he got there and it took another bullet to put him down permanently. The second was a three by two points and about the same size as the four point. The last buck was a forked horn with eye guards. My first shot had actually scored his chest which was why he had quit running.

Before the morning was over, pictures had been taken; and the deer had been tagged, gutted and dragged to the bottom of the mountain for transportation back to camp.

It's not every day a hunter gets to bag three bucks in forty seconds or less with a single shot rifle, but the Sheepshead Trio will always be one of the highlights of my hunting trip to eastern Oregon.

SPRING GOBBLERS IN OREGON

As I sat huddled with my back to a giant oak tree, the cool morning air was awakening. Early birds were subtly chirping and rustling about in the leaves over my head. The rosy hue of dawn was directly in front of me, just minutes from breaking over the ridge top. Off in the distance the whistle from a logging yarder and the familiar popping and crackling of a "jake braking" loaded log truck making its first run of the day echoed in soft resonance with the rest of the early morning sounds.

All were familiar and comforting sounds, but not the one I was hoping to hear.

My hunting partner Jerry Camp of Elkton, Oregon and I were out early, hoping to ambush or bag a spring turkey, and the sound I was listening for was their far off gobble answering the hen call.

As dawn broke, brushing the trees and ridge top with her golden light, I heard the first faint far off gobble of a turkey waking up or responding to the call Jerry was using.

The hair rose on the back of my neck and adrenalin surged throughout my body as a second, then a third, then a whole flock of "toms" started gobbling.

"It is probably the same six I saw yesterday," whispered Jerry. "They are up near the top of the ridge, and will be down to feed within a half hour."

Feed in this instance was huge stacks of cut and dried hay filled with oats.

Jerry and I knew an unattached tom that wants to breed and hasn't yet accepted a subordinate role to a boss tom would be ripe for our bogus hen sounds. That goes double for a flock of six jakes he had been watching for the past several weeks.

Early in the breeding season, these young males are seen hanging around in large groups running after every odd hen sound, they hear. Yes, they have foolish lust in their hearts and we were not surprised to hear so many answering gobbles.

Jerry and I are not professional turkey hunters, just a couple of good ole boys who like to hunt. If I had to describe us in a few words, it would be savvy deer and elk hunters, proficient fisherman and novice turkey hunters.

Neither one of us was wearing camouflage nor had our faces painted to look like the surrounding trees and shrubs as you will see on television even though it is highly recommended by the professional turkey hunters.

They say proper clothing is essential. Head-to-toe camouflaged clothing is allegedly ideal, including gloves and facemask. I was told to avoid wearing bright clothing, especially reds, whites or blues, which resemble a gobbler's head coloration, more as a safety issue than for any practical matter.

However, I don't always do as I am told and was wearing a blue polo shirt and blue-wrangler jeans; because I felt safe on this private ranch.

Jerry and I knew to keep movement to a minimum, as turkeys have incredible eyesight. Regardless of our dress, our hunt could have gone the way of the dodo bird if we were seen moving.

It was my first attempt at bagging a turkey and I will tell you now, you will never find me wearing camouflage, when I hunt because I dislike it. Not wearing camo goes back to my days, as an airborne infantry platoon sergeant for Uncle Sam in Vietnam.

In those long ago days, the only individuals who wore camo were Special Forces, and Long-range patrol individuals (LURPS) and rear echelon types from all walks of service. The first two groups deserved to wear camo because their lives depended upon it. The rear echelon wore it because it looked cute and maybe, just maybe they might be confused with a LURP or Special Forces soldier. It is my long held contempt for the latter, which affects my thinking even today about wearing camo even though the war has been over for thirty years

Enough with the politics of the past, lets talk turkey.

Propped across my knees, within easy reach, was a single shot TCR 83, 12-gauge three-inch shotgun loaded with double-ought buck. You might think double-ought buck was a bit severe for turkeys, but rest assured they are tough birds and I did not feel over gunned.

The distance from the oak tree to the haystack was roughly fifty yards and I wanted all the energy I could get to insure I would not wound a bird that might run away.

Earlier I had patterned my shotgun with some so-called turkey loads of number 4 and 6 shot and they did not group as well as my buckshot.

Besides using buckshot is in keeping with my penchant for big bores> Most readers know I consider the 416 Rigby as barely adequate for varmints, so following that logic, buckshot instead of four or sixes would be okay for turkeys.

Jerry and I had earlier agreed we would carry only one shotgun between the two of us. I would be responsible for shooting, and he would act as the lovelorn hen and use the turkey call. If I got lucky, we would move to another location and attempt to duplicate our earlier feat with him shooting and me calling.

Sitting as still as the proverbial mouse we watched the shadows disappear. Jerry would give an occasional light yelping call and instantly the woods would resound with gobbles from the approaching Toms thinking there was a hen waiting for them.

Almost everyone who sets out to hunt wild turkeys during the spring breeding season knows the basic premise - locate a willing tom (s) and call him into shotgun range by mimicking the sounds of a lovelorn hen. It is simple enough, especially if you are inexperienced and do not have your mind filled with images of everything that can, and does, go wrong while dealing with these frustratingly grand game birds.

Ten minutes or more had passed when one of Jerry's yelps was answered from directly over our heads by a real hen.

With a loud rustle and flutter of wings, two hens flew out of the tree we were sitting under and landed by the haystack.

"We are going to get lucky," said Jerry with a smile. "I never knew they were up there."

For the next five minutes or so, Jerry would call, the feeding hens would answer and the still invisible Toms went nuts.

I whispering, "Jerry, I see a turkey in the woods."

"Is it legal," he asked.

"Still too dark under the trees to tell," I answered.

Just seconds later I frantically whispered, "Here they come, here they come."

"I see them, I see them. Be quiet now or you will spook them," admonished Jerry.

Strutting and strolling as though they were the lords of all they walked upon, six gobblers headed our way.

Oregon hunting regulations allows hunters to have one spring tag in their possession. If a hunter is successful, they are allowed to purchase another bonus tag.

"This is going to be easy," I thought. No doubt, it was premature thought, but the idea I might need another tag started running through my head.

The fish and game department sets spring hunting seasons take advantage of the turkey's annual breeding cycle.

What some hunters do not realize is there is a natural progression during the season that dictates the attitude of the turkeys one encounters in the field at a particular time. These vary in timing and scope from place to place, depending on the geographic location, weather, the egg-laying and nesting ritual of hens, and even the amount of hunting pressure in a given area.

A typical spring season can be divided into three segments: beginning or peak gobbling season; middle, subdued gobbling period; and end, another peak gobbling period.

We were hunting in the beginning or peak gobbling period and in one of the premier hunting spots of Oregon.

Though turkeys are now present in every Oregon county, our western portion of the state dominates the scene when it comes to prime turkey land.

It has been rumored some parts of western Oregon hold higher bird densities than anywhere west of the Mississippi. While this may be the case, readers must realize many of these areas are on private land; and Jerry and I were hunting on private land.

A good percentage of birds are behind locked gates or posted fences. However, as bird numbers continue to rise, so to does the level of destruction they wreak on private land. We were working with a landowner who was tired of the birds messing with and on his stacks of hay.

The jakes were a beautiful sight; strutting and strolling they would extend their necks, fan their tails, drop their wings and gobble. Their snoods (the small red nodule above a turkey's beak) would flop about.

One was slightly larger than the others and leading the flock. He was the one I set my sights on.

Whenever their heads were down and I was convinced they could not see me move, I eased my TCR shotgun into firing position.

Letting Mother Nature take over, Jerry stopped calling.

There were two hens feeding by the hay, and six jakes intent on making their acquaintance and or getting something to eat.

They did not appear to be in a hurry but it amazed me how much ground they covered by simply walking. Within a minute or two of being spotted, even though it seemed like hours, I took a bead on the biggest turkey and pulled the trigger.

Bedlam erupted, flying turkeys were going everywhere but one lay silent upon the ground.

It was my first turkey and fortunately, it was with, One Good Shot.

Several hours later and on a different ranch, we again successfully called in some jakes and Jerry also tagged his with, one good shot.

ANTELOPE BY THE BIG LONE PINE

It was on Big Summit Prairie my wife, Sue; son, Joe; and I went antelope hunting. Antelope are quite common in many areas of the West, particularly in the states of Wyoming, Montana and South Dakota, but in Oregon, they are not as common. They can be found in the south central portion and the southeast.

Antelope are so uncommon; Oregon hunters are only allowed one tag per person, every five years. Even then, hunters are not guaranteed a tag. I know of individuals who have applied for 10 years in a row before they received permission from the Oregon Department of Fish and Wildlife to hunt.

Applying for tags is an expensive, and a maddeningly long process in Oregon. To protect the viability of the herds, all mule deer antelope and elk hunting is limited to those who apply and receive permission to hunt. This permission is called a tag and tags are issued by random computer drawings in June.

(Tag applications at $4.apiece) must be received by the ODFW before midnight May 15t. The applicants around June 20 receive successful or unsuccessful notification. It is expensive. A typical family with three hunters (like mine) will spend upwards of $20 per person just to apply. This does not include the$30 for the combination hunting and fishing licenses. However, I will be the first to admit the privilege of hunting with my sons cannot be assessed financially.

John, Joe and I applied for antelope tags; hoping one of us would be successful. It was Joe's first time to apply because he has always been involved with football. Football and antelope season start on the same weekend and he was hoping he would win.

He was excited because the past year, he had gotten his first elk and now he had the opportunity to get an antelope.

Loading up my trusty 19 year old Suburban, (This truck fits me. It's old and battered and as much a part of me as my Contender.) With enough food and water for four days, we headed north and east for the long drive to Big Summit Prairie, where I had killed an antelope many years before. I was hoping to camp at the exact spot I had hunted from before, but I was a little worried I would not be able to find it.

We left the house at 6 am and arrived around 1:30. It's actually a six-hour drive, but we dawdled along the way. We stopped for a mid-morning snack of doughnuts and pop; lunch; and a quick tour of an abandoned gold mine I had discovered on my last hunt.

As I drove past the cut in the road to my old camping spot, I was filled with a sense of relief because I had found the spot I was looking for. Of course, I had to turn around and back track a couple of hundred yards, but it was the spot.

Unloading, we pitched two tents and generally set up dry camp under the sugar pines just yards from the edge of the prairie. The trees provided welcome shade from the hot sun and the cooling breeze of the prairie was just what was needed to make a really enjoyable campsite.

Fire conditions were so bad; thousands of acres of high desert were burning to the North West we had to use propane for our cooking.

By 2:30 or so, we headed out to scout the surrounding countryside hoping to locate some elusive antelope before morning and the opening of antelope season.

We were not very successful. Because I had already spent 7 ½ hours in the truck, I was more anxious to get out and walk than drive around. However, the old axioms of antelope are where you find them is true. They roam in such tremendous circles, driving and glassing is necessary or a hunter may never find them. We did not find any until we returned to our camp and started glassing the prairie, where Sue spotted a herd of 30, comprising bucks and does. They were about 700 yards out into the prairie. The only problem with hunting on the prairie is, it was posted. No hunting, no trespassing, and no firearms. It put us in a tight spot. I had really counted on Joe being able to hunt there. Now I had something else to be anxious about. First, I had worried about finding the right spot to hunt and camp. Now that we were there, what was I going to do to help my son be a successful antelope hunter?

Years ago, when I had hunted the Big Summit Prairie, only portions of it had been posted and with a map, it was possible to hunt upon. We later found out it had been sold and further developed into a huge working cattle ranch. There were literally thousands of cows scattered everywhere, and in the midst of these cows were the antelope.

How do you shoot an antelope in the middle of a cattle herd? The answer is you don't. You hunt elsewhere. Before retiring for the night, Joe and I agreed it would be a good idea to hunt the periphery of the prairie, hoping we would find a Billy on the edge.

Setting my alarm for 5:30, I lay awake wondering where to hunt if we were not successful in the first early morning hunt. By the time I was lulled to sleep by the mooing and bellowing of thousands of cattle, and the wind sighing in the treetops, I still did not have an answer.

Awakening well before 5:30 by cows who thought they were barnyard roosters, I climbed out of my sleeping bag and dressed, shivering in the brisk morning air. I could not but help wish for the hot afternoon sun I had experienced just a few short hours before.

Joe and I left camp on foot, Sue was still sleeping, and we headed for a ridge where we thought he might get a shot on a buck. He was carrying my TCR in 7mm Remington Magnum, the same rifle he used to bag his elk. He is very comfortable using this rifle and I knew if he could see an antelope he would score.

Unfortunately, he did not get to shoot an antelope. There were plenty out in the prairie, but they were so intermingled with cows, it would have been impossible to shoot. It was while we were longingly glassing a huge buck antelope that I heard a shot far off to my right, probably a mile or so away. Because there was only the one shot, I assumed some lucky and skilled hunter had bagged his buck.

Thinking about it for 10 seconds or so, I decided to modify our game plan and headed for the high prairie area, where I thought the shot came from. Antelope are found in herds and if there was one buck there had to be more.

Returning to camp after hunting unsuccessfully for several hours, I fired up the propane, boiled water for hot chocolate and cooked sausage, eggs and toast for everyone. You would have had to be there to understand how nice it was to hold a cup of hot chocolate in that cold morning air.

After eating, we all loaded into the Suburban and headed for the area about three miles away by truck from whence I had heard the single shot.

Within minutes of heading up barely passable dirt in low gear, Joe spotted antelope.

"Dad," he said, "There is antelope by the big lone pine."

Stopping to glass, Sue and I soon saw what he was talking about: a lone doe standing under the tree looking at us.

Assuming if there were one, there would be many, we left the truck and started a slow walk toward the trees, hoping to see more animals.

There were none.

However, I did find the gut pile of a successful hunter. I decided to follow the tire tracks made in the short grass to see if I could figure out from where the hunter had fired. As an avid handloader, I thought I might even be able to find his discarded brass and know what caliber rifle he had used.

While Joe ranged further abroad hunting, Sue and I did some backtracking and I was soon able to discover the approximate place from whence the unknown hunter had fired a 200-yard shot. Unfortunately for me, I could not find his brass, so I assumed he had picked it up.

Returning to the truck, we drove around for several hours, looking for likely spots to hunt, but all we found were large areas of timber and mule deer. We counted 32 deer with the bucks still in velvet. Antelope can be found in the timber, but only along the fringes of the prairie, so we turned and headed back toward the area where we had seen the doe.

Because antelope hunting is so restricted and the area we were in relatively uninhabited, it is customary for people to stop and ask if everything is OK if you are parked alongside of the road. We were parked about 800 yards south of the big lone pine, planning on returning to camp to avoid the heat of the day when a battered old yellow, four-door, four wheel-drive, Ford pickup pulled up behind us and parked.

As I stepped out of my truck to see what was going on, I noticed an antelope head and hide in the bed.

We started talking and I was asked if everything was ok and soon we were chatting like old friends. I asked for and was granted permission to look at the antelope head. It was not long before I figured out one of these guys was the shooter who had killed his antelope up by the big lone pine.

When I mentioned hearing a shot about 6:20 earlier that morning and finding a gut pile around 8 (while pointing toward the pine), the passenger in the truck started smiling and said, "That was me."

Evidently finding his gut pile meant I passed some sort of test, because they became garrulous and shared their entire hunt with us.

They were local ranchers, whose names we found out later were Lee Rhoden and Corn Close. Both were avid antelope hunters and had been scouting the area for days. They knew the location of every antelope for miles around and were willing to share their information.

Lee Rhoden had married a girl from North Bend, Sue's hometown. In fact, Lee's wife's younger brother had been in Sue's class. Soon, Sue and Lee were playing, "Well, do you know," while Joe and I talked with Corn.

I mentioned to Corn that I had looked for his brass wanting to know what he had used to kill his antelope. He smiled, reached into his pocket saying, he was a reloader and he picked up everything he shot. What he showed Joe and me was an empty wildcat cartridge, a 6mm necked down to 22.

We started talking reloading, wildcat cartridges, and our

conversation subtly steered by me, drifted into where would you advise us to hunt?

Corn asked if we had a map, offering to show us some other areas to hunt. Getting out our map he circled the spots he would have hunted if he had not already tagged an animal. We talked about the herd they had hunted and Corn told us there were still 3 nice bucks and about 20 does.

His advice was to hunt in the other areas he had marked on the map today and if we were not successful to be back in this area the following morning by 6:00 because the herd would be back.

We continued to visit awhile before finally shaking hands goodbye and going our separate ways.

For us, this meant hunting the areas marked on the map.

No luck.

We hunted hard and wide, finally returning to camp around 2:00 to get out of the hot sun, drink Mountain Dew, and eat one of my favorite sandwiches, ham and cucumber for lunch.

We spent the rest of the afternoon listening to the cattle lowing while glassing the plain.

By now the antelope had grazed so far out into the plain they were almost impossible to see, even with my 20X Bausch and Lomb spotting scope. The heat mirage became so intense the antelope appeared to be wavering all over the landscape.

Around supper time we took another run up towards the big lone pine hoping the herd, *Corn* and Lee had told us about had returned. No luck for bucks, but we did see another doe.

Returning to camp, just before dark, I grabbed my folding chair, the spotting scope, binoculars and the latest copy of *"American Handgunner"* and went down next to the wire, posted with its no hunting signs, to sit, read and glass the plain. It looked as if we were done for the day.

As Joe was putting the TCR in the gun case for the night, a large buck antelope, pursued by a cow, came running off the plain toward our camp.

Bedlam prevailed as I dropped my magazine and scrambled to find my binoculars that were hanging around my neck. I started whispering to Joe, "Buck! Buck! Get your rifle! Get your rifle!"

Naturally, the zipper on the gun case stuck. Naturally, the

buck decided to lay down not more than 250 yards away and there we were, without a rifle.

It took only seconds, but the buck was up and away, unwilling to put up with the cow that had reappeared, wanting to play.

By now, Joe had his rifle and I my binoculars (which were never lost), and we stood, rather sadly, watching him run out of range and back into the huge herd of cattle.

The early morning stars were giving away to sunlight as Sue, Joe and I sleepily climbed into the Suburban and headed out for another day's hunt.

Conversation was limited as I tuned the radio to an oldies station, playing, "*Duke Of Earl.*"

I was a little concerned. We only had one more day to hunt and I really wanted Joe to tag an antelope. My concern was not necessarily a do-at-all-cost type of feeling. It was more on the line of, is there anything else I could have done to help?

Reaching our barely passable track heading out through the sage and sand, I shifted into low and slowly started driving toward the big lone pine.

We had only gone 200 yards or so when Joe said, "Hold it, Dad, I think I see antelope."

I started glassing and could not see a thing.

"Talk to me, Joe," I said as I continued to glass, "Tell me where you are looking."

"Dad! Dad! I see them!" He said excitedly, "There are antelope by the big lone pine."

Sure enough, I could see 20 or 30 antelope including three bucks, feeding near the tree, which was more than 600 yards away.

Speaking very quietly, Joe and I discussed the best way to approach without spooking them. We decide it would be up through a long narrow ravine that bisected the field.

Patting Joe on the shoulder I said, "Go for them, Joe, they are all yours."

It was very hard for me to sit and watch him make his approach. There were times I thought he was going too fast, others when he could have stooped a little lower and gone slower.

I also felt a great sense of pride as he got within shooting distance without spooking the entire herd.

By now, the antelope were starting to get edgy and were continually looking toward Joe and then turning to look at the distant tree line. Closer examination with the spotting scope showed two other hunters, one wearing a blue coat lying in wait in the tree line.

Glassing back to Joe, I saw him crouching behind a small tree using one of the branches as a rest. He was aiming at a buck that was standing broadside to him about 250 yards away.

"Take your time, Joe. Take your time," I muttered under my breath.

Seconds went by and no shot. Joe stood, crouched, re-aimed, and stood again but still he did not fire.

"Hmmm," I thought. "He must be concerned about his field of fire."

Later, I learned he had buck fever so badly he could not hold his rifle.

Crack! His TCR fired.

"Damn, he missed," I said to Sue, as the herd made a frantic run for the tree line.

Then I saw a buck fall, and stagger up, badly wounded, as it tried to follow the herd.

"He's wounded one," I said to Sue.

Joe, thinking he had missed was about to take another shot, when he saw the buck fall before it scrambled out of sight. Grabbing his rifle and taking off at a dead run he soon at the wounded buck back into his sights.

Hearing another shot, I said to Sue, "Stay here. I can't stand it any longer. I am going to go help. Watch and if I wave from that hilltop," pointing, "I want you to bring up the truck."

For an old man, it did not take me long to cover the distance to where I thought Joe might be. As I topped the hill, I saw the hunter in the blue coat congratulating Joe by shaking his hand.

Turning, Joe saw me and said, "Hey Dad, I got him."

The blue-coated hunter said, "You've got to be real proud of that boy. He's a hunter."

"Thanks," I replied. "I am."

By now, I was close enough to Joe to be enveloped in a bear hug strong enough to make my back crack. "Good job, son," I said. "I'm proud of you."

Our successful hunt was over and for the rest of my life, I will always remember this particular hunt and the excitement I heard in Joe's voice when he said, "Dad, there is antelope by the big lone pine."

TWO ELK DOWN: "WHO KILLED THEM?"

In order to protect the viability of western Oregon's elk herd the state has chosen to divide the elk hunting season into two parts. Individuals wanting to hunt have the option to apply for first season tags which are good for five days, or they may apply for second season tags which last two weeks.

The premise is second season should be longer because the elk are much more wary and alert having been hunted during first season.

Historically first season hunters are more successful than second so in order to be fair and to extend our hunting season my hunting party was divided between those who had received tags to hunt the first season and those who received tags to hunt the later and longer second season. Our party of eight hunters always splits the seasons and the tags which means if you had a first season tag last year you will have a second season this year.

Sounds confusing and complicated but it isn't and more importantly it is considered fair. Hunters who do not have tags are expected to be out in the woods dogging, meaning working, for the successful tag applicants.

Those of you who are successful elk hunters know getting a huge animal out of the woods is extremely difficult and the more hands available for dragging, quartering and or backpacking the easier the job becomes in getting your animal to the locker.

Opening morning found Jack Fearell, Jeremy Bourell, Joe Bourell, Ben Ferguson, Dave Pappel, Bruce Bennett, Rick Spring and me in downtown North Bend, Oregon at Mom's café eating breakfast and discussing the who's and where's as we developed the game plan for the days hunt.

Jack, Ben, Dave and Jeremy all had first season tags. In our planning it was decided that I would take Bruce, Ben, Joe and Jeremy with me to check out a ridge on the Kentuck side of Willanch where we knew elk could be found.

Rick, Dave and Jack would scout another ridge that paralled the one that my party would be hunting. We knew from past experience both ridges supported herds of elk and it would be a matter of finding them before hunting.

Promising to pick Ben up at the bottom of a long timber covered ridge, I dropped him off and then drove Jeremy and his Dad Joe to another whose terminus was close to Bens.

Bruce and I then drove some adjoining roads looking for fresh elk sign while keeping our ears tuned to the little Motorola radios we all carry in order to stay in touch.

Approximately and hour and a half after dropping the guys off, I picked them up at the bottom and heard them both say, "Lots of fresh sign but no elk."

As we headed towards still another ridge to look for elk, I received a message via the radio that Rick wanted me to join him with a tag bearer as fast as I could because he had spotted a branch antlered bull feeding in the reprod. (Reprod is forester talk for reproduction, meaning young growing timber).

Because Jeremy and Ben had the tags they jumped into my truck and we headed towards Ricks position as fast as we safely could. Joe was left to find his own way back to his own pickup.

Twenty or thirty minutes after Rick called, I stopped and pointing towards a cat road, told Jeremy and Ben to move out as fast as they could and that Rick would be waiting for them on the top of the ridge.

Because we are old gray haired geezers Bruce and I followed at a much more leisurely pace carrying our binoculars, range finders, cameras and other miscellaneous gear elk hunters pack.

As we walked up the cat road, I listened for a shot indicating someone had filled their tag but never heard one and soon we could see Rick, Jeremy, and Ben all glassing off the ridge top down into a huge clear-cut filled with ten year old reprod.

Holding his forefinger to his lips indicating silence Rick whispered that he had seen a branch antlered bull feeding in and out of the reprod for the past twenty minutes but that it had disappeared.

"Where are Jack and Dave," I asked?

"Jack is on the next landing," he replied. "Pointing he said, "Dave is down there at the bottom of that clear-cut below the elk I spotted."

Whispering, I told him I was going to go find Jack.

Heading up still another cat road I met Jack coming down.

"Go back, go back," I frantically whispered. "There is a bull elk just around the corner in the clear-cut. Jeremy and Ben are trying to shoot him if they miss he could run right by your position."

Without saying a word he turned and hurried back to his viewpoint over looking the clear-cut.

Lying down along side him to remain hidden as much as possible I brought him up to date on the fact there were no elk on the ridges we explored and that Rick had asked me via radio to bring the two guys over.

Jack then related that for the past hour or so he and Dave had watched eight cow elk and two spikes feed in and out of the clear-cut but that they had not seen any legal bulls.

Appraising our situation I suggested Jack should move from his present position and go down about fifty feet which would give him a better command of the clear-cut and a better opportunity to shoot if a legal bull should run by him.

As he moved downward we both heard a single shot from the direction of Ben and Jeremy.

Minutes passed and not a sound from anyone.

"That is a funny looking stump," I thought. "It is really light."

Glassing, I saw antlers, and a rump and a body. I was looking at a bull elk. My God that's not a stump, it is a legal bull.

"Jack, Jack," I whispered frantically while pointing. "It's a bull, it's a bull, shoot him."

"Where, where," he replied, "I can't see him."

Frantically he turned and made his way back up the ridge, for a better viewpoint.

"There, right there."

Glassing, I watched the bull as he turned his head to look back over his shoulder trying to figure out what all the commotion was about on the ridge top.

"Crack," Jack's .309 JD Jones Contender Carbines fired.

The bull disappeared and several cows went over the ridge.

Down the mountain side I could see Dave tucked in behind a huge stump looking up at us and wondered why he didn't fire at the bull that had just gone over the ridge.

"What do you think Jack, did you get him?"

"I don't know it was a good shot."

We waited a few minutes and then Jack started down the ridge as I guided him to where I saw the bull disappear.

"Wait a minute, wait a minute," I cried, "there are two more bulls right where yours disappeared."

Instantly they were gone.

"What's wrong with Dave why isn't he shooting," I wondered? "He must be able to see the elk coming off the ridge."

About ten minutes after Jack was slowly making his way down the ridge, we heard Dave fire his .309 JD Jones Contender Carbine.

"Talk to me Dave," I said into my radio. "What do you have?"

"I got a bull," he replied. "There was one standing with blood on his left hind quarter, I shot him and he's down."

Bulling his way through the last huge patch of wild blackberries, I told Jack he was almost on the spot where I had seen his bull disappear and that by moving a little to the right he should be able to see his bull.

"No Charlie," said Dave over the radio. "He needs to go more left. I'll guide him from here."

"Understand," I replied and moved off, back down the cat road to find out what was going on with the guys who had fired the first shot.

Ben was down in the clear cut looking for the elk he had shot. Rick, Bruce and Jeremy, were all pointing in different directions where they thought he should be looking.

Knowing from past experience that the shooter should always be the one to guide others to the area where they think game might be, I told Ben to come back up and let someone else go down and look for his elk.

Jeremy volunteered.

Dave came on the radio to announce that Jack had found their bull and that it was a five point.

Jack and Dave started field dressing their elk. Joe stayed with Ben and Jeremy to help Ben find his missing bull. Rick, Bruce and I walked back down the hill to recover the trucks.

Fortunately for everyone there was another cat road at the bottom of the clear cut which would allow us to get close enough to the elk to use some 5/8 inch line and a pulley in order to drag them out whole.

As I was hanging the block (pulley) on a large cedar tree, we all heard Jeremy announce that he had found blood and was following the trail.

Rick took the rope I had threaded though the block and his machete and started cutting his way up the hill towards Dave and Jack.

"The blood trail is leading right to Jacks bull," I heard Jeremy yell. "Here he is; I found him; it's a five by four bull."

With the muscles of Ben and Jeremy and six hundred feet of 5/8 inches nylon rope it was still over two hours before we had the elk down into the road where they could be loaded into our trucks.

Grabbing the horns of the light colored bull I said to Ben, "That's quite a bull Jack shot."

"That's not Jacks, he replied. "That is the one I shot and tagged. Jack and Dave doubled up on the other and Dave tagged it."

I was confused; I could have sworn the light colored bull was Jack's. After all it looked just like the one I was glassing when he shot. But I was not in the woods when they found them and they should know better than I who shot what.

Shouldn't they?

Pictures were taken, hands were shaken, and congratulations offered.

Returning home after skinning and quartering the two bulls and putting them into our walk-in cooler I could not get the shooting sequence out of my mind.

Particularly irksome to me was who had shot what? The scenario in my head did not make sense with what I was being told about who killed what elk.

"You know Sue," I said to my wife, "They think they know who killed the bulls but I think they're wrong."

What do you mean?

"I am not sure," I replied. "There is just something strange about the shooting and tagging this morning, I'll just have to think about it."

Throughout the rest of the day and evening, I played and replayed the day's events in my mind, but still no definitive answer.

Awake at two the following morning I finally figured out what was bugging me.

Remember when I told you that I wanted Jack to move further right when he was looking for his elk? And Dave said no he needs to go further left and let him guide Jack to his/their bull? That is the point that was bugging me. Jack's bull could not have been further left if it had died as I think it had when he pulled the trigger.

Therefore the bull Dave shot, had to have been wounded by Ben.

Let me explain.

Jeremy found a blood trail and earlier had said, "It is leading me right to Dave and Jack's bull."

I knew both bulls had crossed the ridge top in exactly the same place because I saw them minutes before Dave had fired. As Jeremy followed the blood trail, he literally stumbled across Jack' elk which was lying dead less than twenty feet to the right of the first bull and everyone assumed it was Ben's bull.

As we skinned the light colored elk it was easy to see that the shot placement was perfect on the light colored bull. It was exactly where it should have been if it had died from Jack's bullet.

Ben was always unsure whether or not his shot was good. His witness Rick, and Jeremy knew he had hit one, because they heard the sound of the bullet striking. The question I had was, whether it had been a fatal shot.

As the hide came off the other elk it was plain to me a bullet had entered the elk's left hind quarter at an angle that would support my premise it had been fired by Ben. It would have also been impossible for Jack to have hit the elk at that angle because he was not in position, and Dave's bullet entered the rib cage

Now I had to convince the other hunters that what had been bugging me all afternoon, evening and well into the wee hours of the morning was the true story of who had killed what elk.

As we gathered in Mom' Café for breakfast, I instantly had everyone's attention when I quietly said, "I have a story to tell you about yesterday's hunt. One of you did not kill an elk like you thought you did and when I am finished I'm sure you'll agree."

So I related the story I just told you. When I finished even Ben agreed it was his bullet that had wounded the elk that Dave killed.

Thus ends; TWO ELK DOWN: "WHO KILLED THEM?"

"CHARLIE, I'VE SPOTTED SOMETHING"

Those words, spoken by my brother-in-law Jack Fearell; were about to send me out the door of my pickup and on to one of the most exciting and fulfilling hunt for antelope I have ever experienced. We were just to the east of Big Summit Prairie that my wife, Sue; Jack; his wife Mary Jane; and I were hunting.

Antelope are quite common in many areas of the west, particularly in the states of Wyoming, Montana and South Dakota, but in Oregon they are not as common. They can be found in the south central portion and the southeast.

Jack and several other hunting buddies and I always apply to the Ochoco unit in order to accumulate points for a successful draw. It took me nine years to be successful this time and at the rate he's been applying my brother-in-law should get a tag in the next six years.

Loading my fifth wheel trailer with enough food and water for seven days and hooking it up to my Dodge pickup, I left in a caravan with Jack and Mary Jane to a campground just off Big Summit prairie called Deep Creek.

It is a long 319 miles and seven hours of driving to Deep Creek where we set up camp.

We arrived two days before hunting season because we wanted

to scout for antelope. As they are creatures of habit if you can spot them in an area on a particular day they should be in the same place when it comes time to hunt.

This was my third trip hunting in the area and the first time I had ever had the luxury of camping in a trailer.

In the good old days a pitched tent and some propane would have gone a long ways towards my creature comforts, but as a testament to my old age I really like sleeping in a queen sized bed, having a flush toilet and large refrigerator filled with pop, cold cuts, bacon and eggs to help soothe the aches and pains.

As I drove past the cut in the road to my old camping spot, I was filled with a sense of nostalgia because it was the place where I camped when I killed my first antelope years ago. It was where we camped when my son Joe killed his antelope.

There was also nostalgia for old hunting partners who are no longer with us. Orville Bird and my father–in–law John Emmett who hunted antelope with me on two other occasions, have both passed on.

Unhitching upon arrival was done in 93-degree heat. Rather warm for a guy used to cooler coast weather.

Fire conditions were bad, thousands of acres of high desert were burning to the north, and the air was full of smoke.

By 4:30 or so Jack and I headed out to scout the surrounding countryside hoping to locate some elusive antelope. We were not successful, because we had already spent 7 ½ hours in the truck, we were more anxious to get out and walk than drive around. However the old axioms of antelope are where you find them is true. The driving and glassing is necessary or a hunter may never find them.

We did not find any until we returned to the Big Summit Prairie area, which is a huge private ranch. Because it is private, it is posted every sixty feet with the following admonitions: "No Hunting, No Firearms, This Area Is Patrolled, and We Will Prosecute Trespassers."

On the ranch there are literally thousands of cattle scattered on the prairie and in the midst you can see antelope. Comprised of bucks (Billies) and does they were anywhere from two hundred to two thousand yards out into the prairie. They were fun to look at but off limits.

Jack and I scouted for two days and during that time never saw what I would call legal antelope which meant that I was unsure as to where we would go opening morning.

The night before opening day as we sat around talking and watching bats flit overhead, I told Jack we might as well go to the area where Joe had killed his buck five years before. After all we might get lucky.

Jack set the alarm for 5 a.m.

I could not sleep. Before opening day jitters had me tossing and turning most of the night. I lay awake wondering where we would go if we were not successful in the first hunt. By the time I was lulled to sleep by the wind sighing in the treetops, I still did not have an answer.

Awake and out of bed by 4:30, I shivered in the early morning air as I put on water to boil for a cup of hot chocolate. Most of you who are hunters know how nice it is to wrap your hands around a hot cup in the cold morning air.

As I sipped my chocolate I wandered around outside looking up at the brilliant stars and slow moving satellites waiting for five o'clock to arrive so I could wake Jack.

The early morning stars were still sparkling like sunlight on ocean waves as Jack and I sleepily climbed into my truck and headed out for the big lone pine area to see if antelope had shown up during the night.

Conversation was limited as we listened to a CD of Conway Twitty singing, It's *Only Make Believe*.

Within minutes of departing camp we reached our barely passable track heading out through the sage and sand, I shifted into low and slowly started driving towards the big lone pine.

We drove about three hundred yards and stopped within feet of the same place I had parked when my son Joe had killed his buck five years before. We started to glass hoping that antelope would be out feeding. Even though the stars were still shining it was light enough to see.

Ten minutes or more went by when Jack said, "Charlie I've spotted something."

I continued glassing in the area his binoculars were pointing and could not see a thing.

"Talk to me Jack," I said as I continued to glass, "Tell me where you are looking."

"Way beyond the big pine right up next to the timber. There is something feeding."

Sure enough, I spotted an animal grazing and slowly moving towards our position.

"Looks like a deer," I said.

"Yeah you could be right, but it is so far away let's give it awhile to make sure."

As the sky brightened Jack said, "Charlie that animal is too light to be a deer. I think it's an antelope."

Glassing again, I could see he was correct.

"I am out of here," I said as I opened the door and stepped out of the truck. "I'm going after him."

"What do you want me to do?" asked Jack.

"You stay with the truck and let me know what he does," I replied.

Picking up my single shot Encore rifle in 7mm Remington Magnum, I slipped a cartridge into the chamber, grabbed my binoculars, hand-held radio and moved out.

Moving quickly and quietly through the short sage I slipped into some timber that I knew would bring me within 400 yards of the antelope if he did not get spooked and move.

Several minutes passed when over my hand-held radio I heard Jack say, He's definitely a legal buck and he is feeding towards the south.

Using a radio technique I learned in Vietnam, I broke squelch twice to let him know I understood.

"He's spooked he's running, he's headed south, towards the lone pine," said Jack.

"Click, click," I replied.

"Crack," someone fired a shot off to my left.

"Someone is shooting at him," I said to Jack.

"No," he replied. "It's in the wrong area."

Reaching the lone pine, there was no sign of the antelope.

"Jack," I radioed. "I'm at the lone pine and there is no antelope around here."

I later learned that even though Jack and I had been looking at and discussing the lone pine while scouting, what he thought I meant by the lone pine is not what I meant by the lone pine. In fact our respective trees were almost eight hundred yards apart.

"I can see him," he replied. "He's off to your right, over in the area where Joe shot his."

Click, click. I replied.

Glassing, I soon picked up my antelope about four hundred yards away. I could tell it was a legal buck (horns longer than his ears) but trying to shoot him was impossible because there were trees between us.

Sneaking closer I finally got into a position where I could shoot.

"Too small," I thought. "His horns are only a couple of inches above his ears."

As he stood there looking warily around, I once again quartered his chest with my cross hairs.

"No," I thought, "too small."

"Jack," I radioed, "He's too small and I am going to let him go."

"Okay," he replied. "But he looks big enough to me."

"Well I hope I don't live to regret it."

About then he took off at a run leaving me feeling a little sorry I had not shot him. As he was running his horns appeared to grow larger and I was filled with even more remorse that I had passed him over.

The best thing I could do was to get as close as possible and really scope him out. He had disappeared below the crest of the hill so I knew I could get closer without spooking him.

Moving at a quick crouch I headed for the spot where he had disappeared.

As I crouched, I spotted movement off to my right and a long ways away. Stopping to glass, I could hardly believe my eyes there were three more bucks running just south of Jack. They appeared so close he could have hit them with a rock.

"Jack, Jack," I whispered frantically, "There is antelope behind you."

They quickly ran out of my sight.

"Charlie," I heard. "The last one is big and they are coming your way."

I immediately sat down and started glassing the horizon hoping they would turn and come my way.

"Crack," a shot rang and then another in the direction they had gone.

Feeling a little sick that someone was shooting at my antelope I jumped to my feet and ran in the direction of the shots.

I had covered about 100 yards when I saw black horns coming my way. The ground was so sloped that their bodies were not visible and I knew they could not see me.

"Take the last one," I heard over the radio. "He is the biggest, the last one,"

Again I sat down and waited for them to come to me.

Glassing I could see there were still three bucks running full tilt. The biggest was about fifty feet behind the other two.

Steadying my 7mm Remington Magnum Encore against my shoulder, I placed the cross hairs just in front of what I thought was the last buck.

Fortunately for me the horns didn't look right. They were not as big as I thought they should be. Looking again through my binoculars, I realized I had drawn a bead on the middle buck.

"Oops wrong one," I thought.

Now they were about 100 yards away and coming fast.

Taking another bead on the last buck, I led him by placing the crosshairs just in front of his shoulder.

"Crack; thwock I heard the bullet strike.

He accelerated and caught up with the other two bucks who had also hit high gear and were fast leaving the area.

I could tell he was hit; he was running flat out in a funny way.

Frantically I reloaded, took a bead and again pulled the trigger.

Thwock; again I heard the bullet strike.

This time he tumbled and rolled end over end several times and then lay still.

Taking a deep breath to calm my rushing nerves and to quell my shaking hands, I quietly radioed Jack and said, "Jack I just killed my antelope."

In a short while Jack arrived and we took pictures and congratulated one another. My shaking hands calmed as the adrenaline coursing through my veins dissipated.

Calmed enough so I could gut my antelope and prepare him for capping. While working Jack told me the shot I had heard, which turned the antelope my way, was someone who shot the first buck I was chasing.

Our successful hunt was over and for the rest of my life I will always remember the excitement in Jack's voice when he said, *"Charlie I've spotted something."*

Bruce Bennett, Dennis Weehunt

Charlie and a NH moose

Charlie and his sons Joe and John

Charlie and his brother Ed

Charlie, father-in-law John and son John

Dave, Dennis, Jack, Mike, Justin, Becca

Jack and his son Jeff

Eastern Oregon Hunting Camp

Joe, Dave, Ben, John

Joe, Justin, Dave

John, Earl

My sons John and Joe

My son John and wife Sue

Red, Rick, Orvel, John

Rick and my son Joe

Rick, Charlie, Joe, Red, Dave, Dennis, Justin, Becca

My brother Steve and his son Jamie

"GOT AMMO?"

After months of idyllic weather, the Oregon Coast was being drenched in the first of the winter's storms. Twenty–two foot-high, storm-generated swells produced a deep rumbling sound that I could hear from more than three miles away. The pounding of the relentless surf created by these monster swells created a constant roar that I used as a guide at my back as I climbed a steep ridge in the darkness. The rain-soaked ground made climbing difficult as I worked to get to the top before daylight. It was Sunday and the second day of Oregon's Roosevelt elk season and my hunting partners and I were once again pursuing elk.

Saturday, opening day, had been a bust. We saw cows and some bulls with spike antlers, but our season and area of hunting (Tioga Unit) required three points or better before they are considered fair game and legal.

We had hunted all day in the wind-driven rain and became soaked to the skin. I don't care what advertising companies say about their rain gear being waterproof in any weather. I am here to say, "Oregon Coast rainstorms will prove them wrong." Even my Canadian Danner boots felt damp when I finally returned home and needed to be put on the boot dryer for a few hours.

Our first place to hunt had been predicated on early season scouting. Several days before the season started, several large bulls had been seen feeding with a small group of cows in the Sumner area. Because they had been seen off and on all summer and we knew they had survived bow season, it is where we spent a fruitless day looking for them.

On Sunday, over breakfast at Mom's café, we decided to return to Willanch area just minutes from downtown Coos Bay.

For the past several years, our hunting party has remained unchanged with the exception we are all older and I am now one of the oldest. My hunting buddies on this particular day were Rick Spring, my hunting partner of 34 years; Dave Pappel, whose nickname is Tracker Dave, friend Bruce Bennett; my sons, John and Joe; and a former classmate of Joe's, Ben Ferguson.

Over the years, we have all killed bulls in the Willanch area, so we returned on Sunday with high hopes, knowing if elk were there, they would be in the reprod (short for reproduction, an area of new trees growing very closely together and usually 4 to 15 feet tall) trying to avoid the wind and rain.

Our first daylight drive proved fruitless. The reprod held lots of blackberry vines and fir trees drenched with tons of water, but no elk, which meant we returned to our trucks scratched and soaked but undaunted and ready for another drive down another ridge just a few miles away.

Imagine a large rectangle comprising of timber, clearcuts and reprod about a mile across. John, Joe and Ben were to go to the far right side of the rectangle in the timber and push off across country looking for elk and or elk sign. Rick and Dave were to go down the middle, which was predominately reprod, find some advantageous view points and wait for the boys to push toward them. Bruce and I went down the left side, which was a new clearcut but overlooked reprod to our left. When we reached the center of the rectangle, we were to push our way toward Rick and Dave.

Bruce did not have a valid elk tag, so he was not armed. He was along to help in the event we needed an extra set of hands and more importantly, to dog the brush, meaning push the reprod like an old-time beater.

Just after 9 a.m., as we scattered to our assigned hunting units, it quit raining and the sun peaked through scattered clouds.

Before locking the truck, I loaded my 7mm Encore rifle,

pocketed three extra rounds and put the ammo case with the leftover 16 rounds on the floor boards. Locking up and telling Bruce where I had stored the key we headed south following a deer trail which weaved its way through salal, blackberries and small reprod to get to the top of the clear-cut where it was our job to go through looking for fresh elk sign.

In minutes, probably ten or so, we were into the clearcut and slowly moving down the ridge, constantly alert for elk.

As I moved past a huge brush pile of logging debris, something caught my eye in the reprod to the left. Hissing at Bruce to stop, I raised my binoculars to glass whatever it was that had caught my eye.

"I see it! I see it!" exclaimed Bruce, as he crouched behind the debris pile to get out of sight.

"Elk!" I whispered. "It's a bull!"

Glassing, heart accelerating and pulse pounding, I could tell it was a bull feeding. I could not tell if he was legal, but I could see one straight antler tine. Hidden behind the brush pile, I continued to scan and watched as he turned his head. My heart went into overdrive, because I could now see many white tipped antlers.

"He's legal," I whispered.

Picking up my hand-held radio, I quietly alerted all of my hunting partners by saying, "I have spotted a legal bull."

Alerting my partners was done out of courtesy and to let them know in the event that I missed or if there were other bulls around, they would at least be prepared and would also know it was me that had shot.

Taking two of the three cartridges out of my pocket I handed them to Bruce, "saying I probably won't need these but if I do, just hand them to me."

Taking a deep breath to calm my nerves, I balanced my Encore on a small tree sticking its way out of the pile and took aim on the bull standing broadside in the sun dappled reprod about 200 yards away.

Slowly, oh so slowly, I squeezed the trigger until the rifle's crack surprised me when it went off.

"Ka Whomp!"

I heard the bullet strike. It is an unforgettable sound to an experienced hunter. "Good shot," was my first thought, right through the boiler room.

"You missed," said Bruce, as the elk switched ends and started walking toward the near ridge.

The reprod became alive with elk, as a dozen or more jumped up at the sound of the shot and headed for the ridge top. I saw a spike and one more branch-antlered bull, but all I was interested in was the one I shot.

Ejecting and calmly reloading the cartridge Bruce had handed me, I took aim and fired again at the bull making his way out of the reprod.

"Ka-whomp!"

"You missed."

"I can't be," I snapped letting my anxiety boil to the surface. "I'm shooting from a rest."

For the third time, I loaded and for the third time I aimed and fired.

Once again I heard, "You missed."

"I am down to my last shot," I said frantically, wanting to put the bull I just knew had to be wounded out of its misery.

As a single-shot pistol and rifle hunter I can count on one hand the number of times I have fired more than once over 30years of hunting. The three extra rounds I had put in my pocket I considered to be almost excessive, but a necessary burden. I always wait until I am sure of my shot before pulling the trigger. My 7 mm Remington Magnum Encore was sighted in to be 2 inches high at 100 yards and with a rest, I just could not believe I was missing.

Reaching into my pocket I removed my fourth and last round.

Again I was told, "You missed."

I almost went nuts when I heard that. I was at least 20 minutes from my truck, 20 minutes of a steep uphill climb through a muddy clearcut and then through the blackberry patch at the top.

"He's down! He's down!" said Bruce.

Glassing, I spotted my bull down in the reprod about 225 yards away. He was lying directly away with his butt toward me. However, his head was up and he was constantly looking around.

Going to the radio I said, "I have a bull down. However, he is alive and I am out of ammo."

The radio went nuts, with everyone trying to talk at once.

The general tone of their responses was, how could I be so stupid?

Tracker Dave said he was the closest and he would go back to the truck and get my ammo.

Long minutes passed many more unflattering words particularly about my shooting skills and stupidity over carrying just three extra rounds were endured as I waited for more ammo.

Finally I heard from Dave, "I am at the truck and it's locked. Where are your keys and ammo?"

"In the back by the fuel valve and in a red box on the floor," I replied.

Time seemed to have stopped.

Finally after interminable minutes I heard Dave say, "I've got them. Now how do I find you?"

Directions were sent and I waited impatiently worried about the bull.

"Charlie! Charlie! I can't get down to you! I can't get through the blackberries," said Dave with desperation in his voice.

"Keep to the left," said Rick. "It is easier that way."

To save time, Bruce had climbed about half way back to the top in order to guide Dave through the clearcut and I was almost overwhelmed with relief to hear him say, "I can see Dave."

Probably 20 or 25 minutes after I had fired my last shot, I heard the cartridges rattling in the box as Dave hastily made his way to my side.

The bull's head was still up as he continued to look around, not moving and obviously wounded or he would have run away.

My first reaction was to kiss Dave, because I was so relieved to have more ammo and to put my suffering bull out of his misery, but I didn't. I just reloaded and took careful aim.

The bull was still lying with his rear-end pointing straight at me, an almost impossible position to guarantee a killing shot. The only shot that I was absolutely sure of was to shoot him in the head. However, I had to wait until he turned his head.

Unsure of my rest, I picked up and moved about 5 feet and waited for him to turn his head. I intended to shoot him between his right eye and ear. When he looked to the right, I fired.

"You missed," said Dave who was watching through his binoculars. "I think you were high."

Reloading for the sixth time, and taking several deep breaths to calm my nerves, I rested my rifle on a small log and waited for him to look to the right. When he did, I fired.

"Good shot. You got him. He's dead." said Dave.

Relief, sorrow and anger coursed through my body, relief that the bull's suffering was over, sorrow because such a noble animal had to die the way he did and anger for getting myself into such a mess.

My hunting partners were so scattered, it took them almost an hour to arrive and help me field dress him as well as get him out of the woods and into a truck.

Later in the day, when we removed the hide, I was somewhat gratified to discover that I had not been missing when I fired. Four of the six rounds were clustered in a fist size group some even penetrated one lung. The fifth shot was a true miss and the last was in his head.

There were many lessons learned that day, but the most important was never again will I venture into the woods with only three extra rounds, because if I do, I could once again be crying; "Has anyone, "got ammo?"

"TAKE YOUR TIME DAD"

It was a very interesting hunting season for me, because for the first time in 30 years, I did not tag a blacktail buck. Ten years ago or less, I would have been embarrassed or maybe even a little humiliated to admit to all my friends that I did, "tag out" as we say here in Oregon.

Now I am writing and telling thousands of readers that my hunting skills are probably not as sharp as they used to be. Other things are not as sharp as they used to be either. I even noticed this season that on more than one occasion, I was getting double crosshairs in my scope, even though I had adjusted the focal lengths. I remember thinking as I sighted in on a small buck, which I hoped would be a forked horn, "Hmm. Which one of these lines is the correct one to use?" I never did get to find out. It was a spike and not legal

I may as well admit that one weekend I even carried a Contender carbine because I was unsure if my eyes would focus quickly enough with one of my scoped hand cannons in the event I had an opportunity to shoot. The rifle scope does allow for a quicker acquisition.

Fortunately it only took one comment from my hunting partner of 30 years to get back on the Contender handgun trail. He said, "You know, Charlie, I think that is the first time I have ever seen you carry a rifle while hunting."

The very next day, my 28-30 Stevens Contender from Bullberry was back in my shoulder holster. No, I was not upset, embarrassed or humiliated. I think it was because I am older, a little less hungry or a little less needful to prove I can outwit game. I have killed my share of game and I have taught my sons the joys of hunting, so I am content.

But although I am content, I am not quitting hunting or exchanging a hike through the woods for my easy chair. Absolutely not! After all, elk season begins the weekend after deer season closes.

Opening morning of Oregon's five-day, three-point-or-better elk season was cold and foggy. I always complain about the fog, but that morning was fog to beat all foggy mornings. I almost drove off the road a dozen times on the short, 15 minute drive from my house to my favorite elk hunting spot.

There were eight of us hunting that morning: my brother-in-law, Jack, and his son Jeff; Rick, my 30 year hunting partner and his son, Justin; Dave Pappel; Eric Anderson; and me, with my son, Joe. Because Oregon requires that its elk season be divided into two seasons, Dave, Rick, Jeff and I had legal tags. The other guys had tags for second season, which meant they were along to push the timber; hoping one of us would get a shot. Obviously when the second weekend arrives, and the second season begins; they hunt and we push, or as we call it "dog," for them.

We had put the herd to bed the night before and my pulse was racing as my son and I eased our way into the timber shortly before dawn. Elk sign was everywhere, the ground was scuffed, beds were visible and tracks led deeper into the timber. We decided to wait until it got lighter and hoped the fog would lift before pushing on. It wouldn't make much sense to spook the herd in the dark. As we waited, Joe and I whispered about past hunting trips and discussed strategy in the event we crept up onto the herd.

The rest of the guys had entered into the timber in different areas in the event the elk had moved during the night. Each hunter convinced that they were on the correct trail and would be the one with bragging rights before the day was over.

As the sky lightened, it remained foggy, but not enough to deter us from hunting. If we had been after deer we would have stayed until it lifted, because deer are so elusive. Elk in herds of 20 or more have more trouble staying hidden.

As I followed the tracks left by the passing elk, I remarked to Joe, "You know, this sign is fresh, but I cannot smell elk." That meant they were good tracks, probably made the day before, but old enough so any smells left by passing elk had dissipated

Joe agreed and within an hour, I knew we were on an old trail. We met up with Dave, who had come into the woods from the opposite direction. Earlier, we had decided if no shots were fired within an hour, we were all to return to our rendezvous point to make further plans. The walk out left me huffing and puffing. I had not realized how steep or how far we had gone into the woods until my lungs started burning.

"This elk hunting is for the young guys," I thought. I wasn't about to tell Joe or Dave to slow down and let me catch my breath; that would be humiliating.

I was carrying my 16 ¼ inch barrel .348 Winchester Encore Carbine that I had Virgin Valley make for me. It was the first time I was using it as a rifle and the second time I was using a long gun for hunting in 30 years.

On the way out, I noticed my rifle starting to feel heavy. I was wishing I had left it at home or was carrying it as a pistol because I could then tuck it into my shoulder holster and get on up the trail. We finally reached the top and the rest of the crew was waiting. After much discussion, we decided to go back into the same timber patch I had just walked out of and do more pushing.

We all knew where there was a bench in the timber where elk hide. It was agreed that Rick and Justin would push to the rest who would scatter along a massive ridge line, which we knew from previous hunting the elk used as an escape route. So with the fog hanging heavy in the air, we all turned and went back into the timber.

It took several hours for us to put our plan into place, but it was a good plan. We were all scattered up and down an old overgrown cat road waiting for Rick and Justin to push through. I had been silently sitting for an hour or so when I heard two quick shots to my left. They were so close together I knew they had to have been fired by Rick. He was the only guy with a semi-automatic rifle.

Yes, he fired. Yes he missed. He later said the elk was so huge and came on so silently and quickly that he spooked. Justin, who had spooked the bull and who did not have a tag, told us later he had watched the bull, a huge 5 point for about five minutes before he was scented and the elk bolted.

We spent an hour looking for blood and other signs that Rick might have hit but could not find any. We decided to call it a day. It was getting dark, the fog had not lifted and there was along walk ahead of us to get to the trucks and our rides home.

I had been hiking up and down hills all day and my hips and knees were creaking by the time I got to the comfort of my truck. Shortly after supper, I was in bed, fast asleep.

At 4:30, the alarm went off and I stumbled out of bed. After banging on the doors of Joe and Eric's rooms, while flipping on the lights, I went to gather up our lunches made by my wife, Sue, and to load the truck.

Our party met at Mom's Café at 5 a.m. to order breakfast and plan our hunting strategy. Mom's is a unique sort of café. In the old days we used to eat at another place until the owner decided not to open so early. We searched around town for another place that would hold a large party of non-smokers and one that would cook our breakfast rather quickly.

Three years before, we had settled on Mom's.

Mom is a lady who is very gracious for our business. She agreed to open any time we wanted her to during hunting season. She normally turns on the grill around 5:30, but I have walked through the door many a Saturday and Sunday morning at 5 to be greeted with a cheery, "Morning, Charlie. The usual?" Did I want my bowl of oatmeal and unlimited coffee? We appreciate her and we tip well for the privilege of eating there.

We decided to go back to the same area to hunt. The sky was clear and the stars were shining brightly as we left the café. I was carrying my 14-inch .375 JD Jones and I was feeling lucky. Today was going to be the day for me to bag an elk. No more rifles for me. All I needed was one of my trusty hand cannons

Shortly after dawn, Joe and I low-crawled across a landing high above a clearcut where we knew elk feed. As we peered over the edge of the landing Joe nudged me and whispered "Elk."

Below us, about 250 yards away, was a huge herd of elk feeding its way to the timber.

My heart went into overdrive.

This was the herd we spent all day yesterday looking for. Just two days before it had nine branch-antlered bulls, seven spikes and 46 cows. It was a big herd. Oregon hunting rules requires to be legal a bull must have a least three points on one of its antlers; hence, the term, branch-antlered bull.

The elk had no idea they were being spied upon. As my heart slowed, Joe and I started glassing to see if we could locate the big bulls. After several minutes, it became apparent that here were no legal bulls with the cows.   Spikes were everywhere but they were not legal to shoot.

"Where do you suppose the bulls have gone," I whispered to Joe?

"They might be feeding just over the ridge to our left," he replied. "I'll go see."

Crawling about 20 feet to my left opened up new vistas and even more elk. This time I thought I could see two branch-antlered bulls. I signaled to Joe to join me, and we discussed whether the two light-colored elk on the far side of the herd were legal bulls. They had their heads down feeding and we could not tell. I knew that three other members of my hunting party had to be glassing the same herd. If they had followed our game plan, they should be off to my right and considerably closer.   However, the terrain was so steep and convoluted in the clearcut they were out of sight.

After several minutes of us intense glassing, the light-colored elk raised their heads and Joe and I knew we were looking at two legal bulls. I was in a quandary.   I knew Eric and Dave had to be closer.   But could they see the legal bulls?   I was 250 yards away and knew that if I shot, the herd would bolt for the timber. We studied the elk for almost five minutes, actually thinking that the other members in our party would shoot.

I started to get anxious. The bulls were now less than 50 yards from the timber and if I did not do something soon, I might not get another chance to shoot.

"Joe," I said, "I am going to shoot the biggest bull and I want you to spot for me."

The bull I picked was now standing straight on from me but a long way away. I dialed up my Simmons 2 x 7 scope to seven power and put the cross hairs directly between his shoulder blades. Because he was looking directly at me I figured any bullet drop would still be fatal.

"Take your time Dad," I heard Joe coaching. "Just squeeze it off."

"The student has become the teacher," I thought.

I was lying flat on the ground. My wrists were being supported by the edge of the landing and I had a perfectly still sight picture. Slowly- oh so slowly- I squeezed the trigger. The recoil as the pistol fired actually startled me. Just before I lost sight of the bull, I thought I saw him hunch.

"You got him!" Joe exclaimed. "You got him! Let's go."

With those words, he leaped about 20 feet down the steep hill saying, "Come on, Dad. Hurry!"

As I followed at a more sedate pace, I saw my bull stagger about 20 feet and fall. With the hills still echoing from my shot, Eric fired and killed the remaining bull as the herd bolted for the timber.

Some minutes later, there were high fives, congratulations and handshakes all around. It turned out Eric could see the bulls but wanted to get as close as he could before he fired. My shot, which he knew had mortally wounded one bull, helped him to quickly decide he had better shoot. Dave knew where the bulls were, but they had fed out of sight, as he low-crawled through the clearcut. My bull, which in body size was the larger of the two, had the smallest set of antlers; a 4 x 4. Eric's bull was a fairly large 5 x 5.

We spent more time taking pictures and reliving the hunt and then the work really began. We had two huge animals to get out of the woods.

Next weekend, my sons have tags. If all goes well I will be dogging for them and maybe, just maybe, I can whisper, "Take your time, son. Take your time," as one of them pulls the trigger on a huge bull I know about, skulking in the woods.

IT'S A LONG WAY TO THE TOP

As I pulled into the driveway just after noon, having returned from Bend, Ore., and the Nosler bullet factory where I had gone to replenish my supply, I could not help but wonder if my oldest son, John, had filled his elk tag while I was gone.

It was Thursday and I had been gone for two days with my wife, Sue. The trip to the Nosler factory was but a small part of our trip east. The main purpose was for us to see snow. It probably sounds kind of funny for those of you who live in snow country to hear of others driving to see it, but we did. We even had to have chains, or in our case, studded tires, in order to get to Bend, but we went anyway.

John had a late-season cow elk tag, one of 10 issued for our county. He was hunting with an arrestor equipped 14- inch .375 JD Jones T-C Contender with a full length TSOB and 2x-7x Simmons scope. Because we didn't have tags, the rest of us left our guns home as we "dogged" for John on Monday and Tuesday. It was on Tuesday when I gave him some bad advice that caused him to miss out on scoring on a huge old cow. We had spotted five elk, two huge bulls and three cows just after daybreak and I had cautioned him not to shoot, figuring we could sneak closer. We tried, they ran and we came up empty-handed.

On Wednesday, my wife and I were halfway to Bend when I remarked, "You know, it would be kind of nice if John got an elk while we were gone. It would be his first without me, and his first with a handgun."

Her response was a typical mom's. "Well, I just hope he is careful. Besides, what are we going to do with another elk? The freezers are already full."

I didn't answer.

As I was unpacking, I noticed there were two messages on the answering machine. I decided I would listen to them after I had unloaded the car.

Usually, the messages are for my sons or someone wanting a family member to call.

When I got around to the answering machine, message number one was someone wanting some reloading information. The second was from my youngest son, Joe, who said, "Dad, it's now 8:15. I was tired and slept in this morning and didn't go hunting with John. He just called from Rick's truck on his cellular phone. He's killed an elk and I have gone to help."

It was a straightforward, simple message, except I didn't have a clue where   they were. As a parent, I wanted to rush out and help. After all, they were just kids.

As I was telling Sue, "John killed an elk," the phone rang.

"Hi, Dad," said John. "I got one."

"Congratulations, where?" I asked.

"Well, you know the big bowl which had all the boulders which looked like elk and where you said, "If you ever see elk down there, don't shoot them. It will take you a week to get them out?"

"Yeah, I remember."

"I shot one down in the bottom of that bowl," he replied.

He went on to explain that he had just packed out the first quarter, and that Joe was there helping. He was calling to ask if I would bring another meat saw. They had broken the one they were using. And more elk bags in which to store the meat.

As I gathered the gear, I could not help but wonder if the general public really understands how difficult elk hunting really is.

For the uninitiated, killing an elk is the easy part. Getting it out of the timber and into a cooler takes a tremendous amount of back-breaking work. Most of the time, they are almost too big for a couple of guys to wrestle around in order to get them into position for gutting. While lying on the ground, the elk then must be skinned, and cut into pieces small enough for a person to carry in a backpack. Once the 100-pound chunks of meat are lashed to pack frames, it becomes a real struggle to climb your way hundred of yards straight up to the waiting trucks.

The first trip is fairly easy. The adrenaline is still high from the kill and it helps boost you to the top. It is the fourth or fifth trip that leaves you gray of face, winded and totally exhausted.

It made me wonder if John was thinking, "Maybe I should have listened to Dad, when he said, don't shoot one down in that hole or you will be all week getting it out."

As I quickly loaded my truck with two meat saws, and hunting stuff, Sue put together, hot coffee, cold pop, water, elk bags, apples, oranges, binoculars, camera, and sandwiches before I headed out. It sounds like I put in a lot of liquids. I did. Back-packing an elk creates a fantastic thirst. I gathered up Grandpa, (my father-in-law,) and we headed east.

Forty-five minutes later, I found the logging road blocked by two trucks. Rick's truck contained some bloody elk bags and I knew I was close to the spot where John had killed his elk.

Down the road where I could glass into the bowl, I saw, way down in the bottom, my sons, with huge packs on their backs, slowly making their way to the top.

"Well, son," I whispered to myself, "You sure earned that one."

I was proud of him; it was his first handgun elk and his first without me.

Kids have a funny way of growing up don't they?

THERE IS A DEER AT THE END OF THE RAINBOW

Blustery blowing weather slapped my windshield as I drove out of my garage, headed for an early morning reunion breakfast at a local restaurant. I was to meet my hunting partners, and we would decide where we were going to hunt for the day.

It was Sunday of the second weekend for Oregon Coast blacktail.

The weatherman had promised local drizzle, followed by brief periods of sunshine and as I drove, I hoped the sunshine would be the rule instead of the exception.

Over breakfast, we found out Jack had left his Gortex Parker riding on the back of his pickup tool box and we would have to return to the area (Willanch) where we had hunted unsuccessfully the day before.

The high price of Gortex did not allow us much opportunity to go elsewhere and we could only hope someone else had not picked it up.

Driving up to my prearranged spot I once again reflected on how this season is so much different then in past years.

Different because I was alone.

Usually there were two or three hunters and their gear tucked in and around my extended cab pickup, but the boys were off on their own.

John was in Corvallis, working for Acres Gaming as a planner buyer for a computer company that writes software for casinos.

Joe was in Eugene, working for Poole Larson in his second year of becoming a funeral director. He was on call and could not get home.

Waiting for daylight, I watched the fog swirl around the cab of my pickup, listening to a tape and wondered how many times had I sat in a pickup waiting for daylight.

"Too many," I mused, as I hummed and sang along with Bob Dylan's, *Corrina, Corrina*.

Climbing into my rain pants and rain jacket in the cramped confines of the cab, I figured the weatherman, as usual, just couldn't predict Oregon's weather as the sky dumped buckets of rain.

"This is a drizzle with partial clearing and some sun?" I thought, as I listened to it pound on the truck's roof. "I'd sure hate to see him make a simple forecast of rain."

I may complain about the rain, but I am smart enough to realize that without it, my little corner of the world would be overwhelmed with people. Therefore, I actually enjoy rain, at list I tell myself I do. After all, where else can one hunt deer and elk 15 minutes from home and be in sight of the Pacific Ocean?

Daylight found me moving west down my assigned ridge. Finding a good observation point, I took time to glass the surrounding country to make sure I could see my fellow hunters and they could see me. Signaling each other we continued our slow decent to the bottom.

As I glassed, the rain started to let up, no doubt to allow the fog that was swirling in to come in unhindered.

Within seconds, all I could see was the dark side of the huge fir stump I was taking refuge behind.

One positive aspect was the rain had stopped and there appeared to be a glimmer in the sky to the east where the sun was supposed to be.

Twenty minutes or so passed and the fog slowly lifted to reveal a beautiful rainbow.

"Guess that weatherman knew what he was talking about after all," I softly said aloud.

A huge and beautiful rainbow arced through the sky from north to south right across the area we were hunting.

The rainbow reminded me of the many times when I was a kid in New Hampshire running through the field after a thunderstorm. Rainbows always appeared and I would run trying to get to the end before it disappeared. Mom or Dad, I really don't remember who, told me I would find a pot of gold at the end if I could get there before it disappeared.

The funny thing was, I could never get to the end. It was always was just out of reach.

"Wouldn't it be something," I thought, "if one of us killed a deer further down the ridge underneath this rainbow?" "Our very own pot of gold in the guise of a blacktail."

Shortly afterwards; the rainbow disappeared and the rain and fog came back.

Once again, sitting behind a stump, I waited for the fog to lift.

A slight breeze soon blew away the vagrant wisps of white and I could see Dave about two 200 yards away hiding behind some downed logs. I knew he was ready to shoot, because I could see his Contender carbine in .309 JD Jones poking out over the top.

Scrambling to my feet, I started down and almost immediately jumped a white muzzled buck, who no doubt had been hoping I was going to spend the rest of the day right where I had been sitting.

He slowly took off headed straight toward Dave as I placed the crosshairs of my 15 inch 30-06 Encore at the junction of his neck and shoulders.

"What a story this will make," I thought; "my first buck with a 30-06 Encore."

"Now wait a minute, there is no need to be greedy," someone said inside my head. "It's Dave's turn."

Reluctantly, I agreed.

Quickly glassing, I could see from his apparent inaction, (meaning the rifle of his carbine had not moved) that Dave had not seen the buck headed his way.

Throwing caution to the wind, figuring I could still kill the buck if I had to, I hollered, "Dave, it's a buck!"

A slight movement of the carbine's muzzle showed my hollering had alerted Dave.

It also caused the buck to pick up his pace, but he did not break into a run.

Continuing downward, and about 20seconds later the buck stopped broadside to Dave standing just 75 yards away.

It turned its head to look back up the ridge, probably trying to figure out who and what had disturbed his early morning nap. Unfortunately, its stopping proved to be the buck's demise.

Dave's carbine cracked and his buck fell rolling down the steep hillside just a few short yards from the spot where two years ago Dave had killed two other bucks.

HUNTING MULE DEER IN EASTERN OREGON

This story got its start when my hunting partners and I opted to give up the month long Western Oregon blacktail deer hunting and applied, under a party permit, to hunt for mule deer in Eastern Oregon's Beulah District.

The Beulah District is a fairly large when compared with all of Oregon's geographic area. It is a little larger than the state of Rhode Island. However, it was not the size that convinced us to try there, but the stories from friends and fellow hunters that it was home to some very large bucks. We were advised to hunt in an area known locally as Sheepshead and Iron Mountains, about 11 miles from the small town of Unity, Oregon, population 23.

Unity is 465 miles from Coos Bay and a hard, nine-hour drive, a long way when there is prime deer hunting just minutes from my front door. But my hunting partners and I wanted the new experience of hunting mule deer.

Deciding we were going to hunt in the Beulah unit, my wife and I and another couple loaded up our travel trailers and headed east, five days ahead of the rest of our hunting companions to locate a camping area that would hold four trailers. More importantly, I wanted to get there early in order to start scouting the lay of the land. Eleven miles out of Unity on Highway 26 and just two miles up East Camp Creek Road, we found a forest service primitive campground, Eldorado. A primitive campground in Oregon means pit toilets, fire pits and no piped water.

Fire pits are important because evening campfires are necessary in order to relive our hunting exploits. It is around a cheerful campfire that our hunting stories are relived time and time again.

Staking our claim in one end of the campground and claiming enough space for three more travel trailers, the Bennetts, our friends who left with us, and the Sharps quickly set up camp and then headed out on a scouting trip down East Camp Creek Road to see if we had picked a good place to hunt. Within minutes, we had seen our first deer does and bucks quietly feeding along side the creek.

Smiling inwardly, I could not help but think it could be my year to bag a mulie.

Within the next three days, as the rest of my hunting partners trickled in from Oregon Coast, we learned what ground was private, what was public and what was closed due to a recent and massive forest fire that had roared through the area in July.

As my partners and I scouted and learned, we debated over the evening campfires the best way to hunt on Saturday's opening morning. By Friday noon, we had a plan that involved splitting our group of six into two teams with my group of three climbing a local mountain called Sheepshead with the intent of hooking up with the other half about 3 miles away.

It sounded good around the fire, it worked well when sketches were made in the ground but opening morning was a different matter.

Getting up early, I was pleasantly surprised to discover my son, Joe, asleep in his car. He had made the six-hour drive from the University of Oregon to hunt with his dad, even though he did not have a tag.

Leaving camp and arriving at our jump-off point more than an hour before daylight, we discovered there were four other trucks parked where I had intended to park. Feeling discouraged, but knowing it was too late to change plans, my son, Bruce Bennett and I headed up Sheepshead Mountain, following a trail by the light of the moon. Reaching the first flat on the mountain about a half-mile from the truck, we huddled behind some fallen trees trying to get out of the wind and waited for daylight.

Thankfully, because we would not have to deal with them, the drivers and or passengers in the other pickups parked at the bottom were not around. However, I assumed they had gone on ahead and any deer in our immediate vicinity probably would have been spooked by their passing, but daylight would tell.

It was a long and cold 40 minutes to daylight. With my nose dripping, teeth chattering and hands cold, I wondered if I could cock the hammer on my Model 95.

Sticking to our original plan to hike to the back side of Sheepshead and meet up with the rest of our crew, Joe, Bruce and I started moving slowly north all the while glassing a huge grass-filled open bowl we were going to cross.

Within minutes, several does quietly exited the area and because they were still around, I quit worrying about the guys in the other trucks parked down below.

Glassing to my right, I saw the largest mule deer I had ever seen standing on a ridge top, nonchalantly posing as if to say, "Well, what are you going to do about it?"

"Joe! Joe!" I hissed. "Look at that buck!"

"Holy cow!" he exclaimed, as he lifted his Bushnell range finder to his eye. "He's 479 yards away, Dad."

"Let's get closer," I said, as I clutched my Model 95 in 35 Winchester tightly to my chest.

Before we could move 100 yards, he spooked and ran off the ridge. Within seconds of his disappearing we heard two shots and later learned he was killed by a first- time hunter. A woman who did not appreciate his measured inside spread of 37 inches.

"Could you have hit him with a scoped rifle?" Joe asked.

"Probably," I replied. ""But I am not sure I would have risked a shot that far away."

We moved on and probably 20 minutes later heard shots off to our front. "Let's sit here awhile," I told Joe. "Maybe they missed and a buck will run over the top of us."

Sure enough, deer showed up.

Three bucks, anyone I would have been proud to hang on my wall but they were quartering away from us running to the west.

"Seventy hundred and forty yards," said Joe, as he lowered his range finder.

"Pretty, aren't they?" I responded.

The rest of the morning was quite uneventful.

We continued hiking toward our fellow hunting companions, some 2-odd miles away along the spine of land marking the top of Sheepshead Mountain. Along the way, we saw more does and at one point, were astounded to see two hunters totally camouflaged including face masks as they sat beside the trail.

I am not one to promote hunter orange but no one hunts with me unless they are wearing at minimum a hunter orange vest and it was our collective opinion that these guys were stupid.

By the time we reached the other guys, we were tired and looking forward to returning to camp. It had been a long day, one full of excitement and I needed a cup of tea and a roll or two to for an energy boost.

Sunday morning, it was cold and crisp with a distinct snap in the air. The weatherman said we were in for possible snow flurries later that day and it was so cold, I was not about to dispute him.

The planned hunt for that morning was for everyone to keep together and encircle a large bowl of the side of Sheepshead, with each of us taking a ridge and slowly work our way to the bottom.

It was a very successful way for us to hunt in back home in Western Oregon because we could see each other ridges and almost entrap any deer that might be in the area.

Probably 20 minutes after starting down my ridge, it started to spit snow.

"Hmmm," I thought. "So much for the weatherman's prediction of snow in the afternoon. He missed it by almost eight hours."

Stupidly, I had left my mittens back in Coos Bay and my hands were freezing. My nose was starting to run and my eyes were tearing from the cold and wind.

Getting behind a large tree to try and avoid most of the wind, I started glassing the ridge line just across from me, the one Jack was pushing down. Wiping my eyes, then my nose with the back of my hand trying desperately not to make any noise especially blowing my nose, I spied a doe feeding about 250 yards away. Instantly I got warm. Or so I thought.

Watching her, I thought she seemed to act funny as though other deer were around but I could not see one and my body temperature slowly slid back into freezing. I got so cold I finally had to get up and move. I tried- believe me-I tried to not be the first to move, but I lost and radioed my partners I was moving.

As I stepped out from behind the tree I took one more look at the doe and was amazed to see she had grown huge antlers since I looked at her last.

"Buck! My God! That is another huge buck," I said to myself, as I once again glassed to make sure I wasn't hallucinating from the cold.

This time, he was looking right back at me, getting ready to bolt if I made the wrong move.

Slowly, I lowered my binoculars and raised the 35 Winchester. Peering through the iron sights, I could not see a thing. The drifting snow, tearing eyes and distance all contributed to my seeing nothing. It was then, I started to regret that I was carrying a rifle with iron sights and wished for my 3 x 9 scoped sighted 7mm Remington Magnum Encore.

Switching between my iron sights and my binoculars, I watched the buck slowly turn and feed off out of sight.

Teeth chattering and body shaking with cold I called my buddies and told them that a huge buck was headed their way and to not let him get away.

He did.

Shots were fired and hunters missed. Somehow, that buck and another three-point he picked up eluded our party and made his way over the next ridge, where he was killed by another hunter. This buck was huge, not as big as the one Joe and I had admired on Saturday, but his rack measured an even 34 inches, huge by anyone's standards.

Monday, the truck's thermometer read 14 degrees as we headed to another valley to hunt. There was a skiff of snow on the ground and my hands were warm and toasty in borrowed mittens. The Model 95 with its iron sights was left in the travel trailer and snuggled into a shoulder holster under my left arm was my scoped 15 inch .270 Encore.

We hunted hard all day but no legal bucks.

That night as I put away my Encore and started packing for the long trip home, I knew I would be back the following year, carrying one of my beloved single-shot rifles made by Thompson Center. Never again would I let an opportunity to bag a world-class buck be stymied by an old-time Winchester.

THERE'S A BULL DAD!

Oregon's, rifle bull elk season starts early in the year, when hunters have to decide, via the application process, on which season they are going to hunt. Oregon has two seasons: an early one of five days and the second, which lasts nine days with a two-day break between seasons.

My hunting group usually alternates from year to year as to which season they will choose to hunt. The first season is usually the most productive for the big bulls, which roam our forested hills, but the period is short with just one weekend and three week days.

We figure alternating it gives everyone an equal opportunity to bag a big bull. Non-tag holders, their season having expired, continue to go afield unarmed to help search for the bulls and, in the event someone is lucky enough to bag one, help retrieve the animal from the woods.

However, a few always opt to hunt the second season.

Second season usually includes Thanksgiving Day and the following weekend. The opportunity to hunt and combine a mini-vacation with relatives is too hard to pass on for many.

My son, John, is one of those who always chooses second season.

He lives in Washington, state and usually comes home for Thanksgiving to hunt. No doubt, the $350 out-of-state tag and license contributes to his wanting to hunt as much as possible, because it ups his chances of scoring a big one.

This year, he arrived on Friday, the day before opening of the second season and Saturday morning, as dawn broke, we were peering into a clearcut looking for elk.

I had already filled my tag, so I was along as the driver, guide and grunt. We hunted hard for three days and saw lots of elk, cows, calves and spikes, but no branch- antlered bulls, the only legal prey.

Our hunting party slipped from 10 guys on Saturday, to six on Sunday. Finally, just the two of us would be hunting on Monday, as time and the requirement to go back to work took their toll.

By Monday, I had been elk hunting for 10 days with a two-day break and the early morning hours and constant searching and climbing up and down steep hills was taking a toll on my 60-year-old body.

When the alarm's strident clang awoke me at 4:30, all I really wanted to do was turn it off and go back to sleep, but my role as father and guide forced me up out of bed and into the kitchen to prepare breakfast.

There would be just the two of us hunting, my son and me, so it was a special day, because I did not have to share my time and expertise with anyone else. There is always something special about a father and son with the common bond of hunting being afield searching, for elk.

The evening before, John and I had decided to go to Coquille to check out some private, gated property (with the landowner's permission) that had a new clearcut. On several earlier hunting forays, we had watched a mixed herd of spikes, cows and calves in the clearcut; feeding and we wanted to return hoping that a mature branch-antlered bull or two had joined them.

We arrived about an hour before daylight and parked about a mile from the edge of the clearcut, knowing a long, quiet walk was better than driving in and spooking any animals that might be feeding.

We sat awhile; quietly reminiscing about past elk hunting trips, and all too soon it was time to leave the warmth of the truck.

We arrived just at dawn, and started glassing the far edge of the clearcut looking for elk, when I said to John, "Do you hear a truck?"

"I think so," he responded, "Sounds like a diesel."

Knowing the driver had to go through two locked gates and had to have the landowner's permission to be there, I was a bit discouraged, thinking it must be another hunter.

Stepping to the side of the logging road, we watched as a three-quarter-ton Dodge pickup pulled up and stopped.

As the driver's face came into view," I facetiously remarked, "Well, so much for quietly walking into here."

"Oh, I am sorry," he replied, as he turned off the truck's engine. "Are you hunting?"

"Yes," I replied, "Are you?"

"No, I have been hired to clean up the clearcut; stack all the logging remains prior to replanting." "That is my machine," he said, pointing to a big yellow tractor called a shovel or loader, parked just ahead of us

"Would you mind giving us 10 or 15minutes to glass the rest of this clearcut before you start work?" I asked.

"Not at all," he replied. "Take all the time you want." "Tell you what, If you get one, I will help you get him out."

Cautiously, we made our way down the "cat trail" headed for an area of high ground, which I knew from previous experience, would allow us to see down into the clearcut. So far, all we had glassed had been the far side, but there were lots of valleys and draws where an entire herd could hide.

Within minutes, almost simultaneously, we spotted a herd of elk.

Instantly we crouched, not wanting to be seen, and started looking for a place to glass the herd.

"Dad!" John whispered excitedly, "There's a bull down there! I saw a bull!"

"OK," I replied, excitement building in my voice, "but let's make sure he is legal. I know several spikes are running with this herd."

"He's legal and he's big," whispered John, glassing the herd from behind a stump.

By then I was in position behind the stump to verify that, yes, indeed, there was a large branch-antlered bull feeding about 350 yards away with 20 or so cows.

"Come on. Let's get closer before you shoot."

As we retreated down the cat road, the shovel operator could tell from our actions that we had a bull in sight.

He smiled and said, "Good hunting, and don't forget, I will help."

John was carrying my Super 14 Contender in .375 J.D. Jones. I say mine, because if I do not, he will claim it as his, having used it to kill four other bulls in his hunting career.

Within a few minutes, we were able to get within 250 yards of the feeding bull and John hiding behind a huge stump was going to use it as a rest for his Contender.

With a racing heart and dry throat, I was hidden behind my own nearby stump, glassing the bull.

"Let me know when you're ready, "I whispered.

"How far?" asked John.

"Two hundred and fifty yards. Hold for the heart." I replied, knowing the pistol was sighted in for that distance.

KABOOM! The pistol roared and the elk flinched.

"You hit him!" I said excitedly. "He's hit hard!"

The rest of the herd ran off into the timber and the majestic old bull with his head down, just stood there, mortally wounded.

Slowly he started downhill, toward the timber and not wanting to lose him, I said, "Hit him again."

KABOOM! Once again, the .375 J.D. Jones sent a bullet smashing into the animal.

The hills were still reverberating with the shot's echoes when the bull fell over, dead.

John had just killed his fifth bull with a handgun and at a measured 253 yards.

The shovel operator was so excited.   "What kind of gun is he shooting? I have never seen anyone kill a bull that far away with such a little gun. Man! Can he shoot"

All of this and more rolled off the shovel operator's lips. I just smiled and thought, "That is my son."

Before leaving with Eric the shovel operator, who volunteered to take me back to my truck, I called Rick Spring, my lifelong hunting buddy to get some additional help. John also called his brother, Joe, to let him know he had just bagged his bull. While I was getting the truck, which had the blocks, (pulleys) and rope we use to get the elk up to the landing for butchering, John went down into the clearcut to claim his bull.

Returning back to the shovel, Eric said the boom would be an ideal place to hang a block. Its height would give us lots of lift, when pulling the elk up and out of the bottom.

A pulley on the end of the boom had a rope threaded through it and then down to the elk's horns. The other end of the rope was tied to the bumper of my truck. With hand- held radios and slow speeds, it is possible to drag a huge animal long distances. The only limitation is the number of blocks and the length of the rope. We regularly carry a, 1200-foot spool in the back of my truck, as well as a mechanical lift used for butchering, which fits into my receiver hitch.

The tremendous lift provided by the shovel made short work out of getting John's bull to the landing. By then, Rick had arrived and we proceeded to butcher the elk, with John taking continually breaks to answer congratulatory phone calls.

I have many fond memories of hunting with my sons and now we had another to share. In the years ahead and while reminiscing around a future campfire I will start this story by saying, "I remember the time John said, 'There's a bull, Dad!'"

ELDORADO DEER CAMP

Deer camps are a thrilling new adventure for new hunters, and a deep-seated passion for the veterans. The traditional deer camp has long been a special event for any hunter. Once a year, families, friends and longtime hunting partners gather at a shack, cabin, campsite, farmhouse, or a special place in the woods on the eve of opening day, to share in the excitement of the upcoming hunt. However, it is not the gathering of friends that fuels the fevered pitch; it is the camaraderie, the talk of big bucks, past successful and unsuccessful seasons, and hunting tactics that all play a role in generating the frenzied atmosphere. Even thought the sights, smells, sounds and camping facilities vary from state to state and season to season, the tradition will always be the same.

Eldorado campground is an unimproved Bureau of Land Management facility located 414 miles from Coos Bay and about 12 miles southeast of Unity, Oregon. Unimproved means there isn't any water or flush toilets, but there are a few picnic tables and fire pits scattered along the banks of East Camp Creek and two outhouses set amongst the ponderosa pines found in that part of Oregon.

The area around Unity is true ranching country, complete with cowboys wearing chaps and riding horses. Our last two trips to the campground have included the sights and sounds of cowboys riding down the road herding their cattle out of leased BLM lands.

Their objective is to protect their cattle from some scissor bill who might not know the difference between a range cow and a mule deer.

The evening before opening day, Eldorado deer camp found a collection of old and new hunters; hunters old in physical years and experience and others new in age without any experience.

Earlier in the year, 14 family and friends applied for a party tag to hunt the Beulah unit of Eastern Oregon. If successful, a party tag means everyone is issued a tag to hunt the same area. It is different from applying as individuals because it is possible for some family members to be successful while a brother, sister, father, or friend could be left without a tag and not able to hunt.

To not be able to participate in a deer camp tradition would be disastrous in my mind.

My wife, Sue, and I took two days to drive the long trip to Unity. We have a small fifth-wheel trailer, which becomes our home away from home when hunting. By the evening of opening day, there were five other trailers parked in the campground.

Soon, there were 15 people sitting in lawn chairs around a huge roaring fire sharing or listening to hunting stories of yesteryear; stories that are similar to those you may have shared with family and friends.

One of the stories told was about the two hunters we had run into the year before on Sheep's Head Mountain, who had all been wearing camouflage, right down to having their faces and hands painted to avoid detection. We were not sure who they were trying to avoid as they were readily apparent to us. As a group committed to hunter safety they appeared stupid in our eyes. We were trying to subtly reinforce to the newcomers if you hunt with us, you are required to wear at minimum, a blaze orange vest.

Many states, including Oregon, do not require hunters to wear any color, but our group feels it is necessary and is very important in keeping track of where we are when out in the woods.

The Sheep's Head discussion eventually rambled into who was hunting where and with whom on the following morning. Before the huge fire died down, plans were finalized to include what truck was going where, and who would be picking up tired hunters in the forenoon of the following day.

Amanda, our newest hunting party member, would be with her dad, Jeff.

Driving up to my kick-off point about an hour before sunrise, my secret spot had two other trucks and four hunters disembarking, all getting ready to head up the same trail I had scouted earlier as being an excellent place to bag an opening morning buck. Slinging my Encore, over my shoulder with its new Virgin Valley Custom Guns 30-inch fluted barrel in 338 Galaxy, I hustled up the trail, wanting to be the first to the top.

Dawn found me alone walking up the trail on Sheep's Head. The four other guys had all passed me as though they were going downhill instead of up. They must have been younger and in better physical condition, but in the dark, I could not tell.

I had originally planned on hunting with my son, Joe, but he never arrived as planned. Tossing and turning throughout the night and not sleeping well, thinking every noise I heard was him arriving from Springfield, Ore., where he works as a funeral director, I was tired and worried and not really interested in hunting.

Where was he?

Before the morning was over, I had seen does, heard some shots, and run into seven other hunters who all thought they were going to have the mountain to themselves. The seven other hunters and the absence of my son made me change plans and I dropped down off the mountain well before the planned-on, rendezvous point.

I met Jeff and his daughter, Amanda, and they took me back to my truck. I went back to camp determined to figure out what had happened to Joe.

At camp, I learned from my wife that he had car trouble and was broken down in the town of Mitchell about two and a half hours west of our location.

Driving into Unity, to find a phone (cell phones didn't work very well in that remote region) to call the garage where he had said he could be reached, we decided we would go get him if his car could not be fixed in a timely matter.

Calls were made and by 1:30, we were headed back down the road to Mitchell. It was a long afternoon of driving, but we returned to camp just before dark in time to participate in the evening hunt.

Two deer were killed on opening day. The first, by Bruce Bennett, a forked horn just after daylight, (one of the shots I had heard) and a small 4-point by Jerry Camp, a newcomer to our hunting group.

Once again, the campfire was roaring and we sat around rehashing the days events, including listening to Joe's story of breaking down in the middle of the night and him having to walk six and a half miles back into Mitchell because no one would give him a ride.

Sunday morning found Joe and me climbing a different ridge leading to the top of Sheep's Head. A single-shot aficionado, I was still carrying my Encore, but Joe had his grandfather's BAR in 30-06. Readers familiar with my stories know that I raised them to hunt with Contender handguns and carbines, but as they got older and more independent, they used handguns, but not as frequently, and Joe wanted to bag his buck using his grandpa's rifle.

We hunted hard most of the day and did not see any deer we wanted to harvest. Several forked-horn bucks and spikes were passed over because we wanted the monster similar to those we had seen last year and we still had five more days of hunting.

Around the campfire on Sunday evening, marshmallows were toasted and with squares of chocolate pressed between graham crackers we made, "smores" a fitting sweetness to end our long, tiring, yet exhilarating day.

Monday was a great day for our group. By evening, three more bucks were added to the hanging tree and because the weather was staying warm, unlike last year's cold and snow, Joe Bourell, who had filled his tag, decided he would leave a day early and take all five deer back to our cooler in Coos Bay.

Monday was also the day I found out that my Leupold 3.5 x 10 A.O. scope would not focus, but on one occasion when I glassed deer some 700 yards away, all I could see was blurry animals feeding on the hillside. I never did find out what happened because everything was okay when I left home, but Leupold has already repaired my scope, one of the reasons I always buy Leupold.

Tuesday morning, I was carrying my Encore in 7 mm Remington

magnum loaded with 175 grain Barnes X bullets and topped with a 3 x 9 Leupold Vari X II scope. This is one of my favorite Encores. I have slowly moved away from single-shot pistols due to an old man's eyesight, which likes to generate double or triple cross hairs leaving me in the predicament of having to guess which cross hair is correct. I grabbed this one because it fits and I am very comfortable with it. Over the past two years, it has accounted for antelope, elk and deer.

Tuesday morning's hunt was a bust if one was to measure it by how many deer were killed. However, we all know hunting is never a bust if one measures being outside, smelling the flowers, listening to the birds, trying to identify new trees and shrubs. I think you know what I mean; at least I hope you do.

When I left camp Tuesday evening, my wife and Amada were accompanying me. The plan was for us to climb a fairly steep ridge up to a bench on the side of a huge natural bowl and then sit and glass for deer while our hunting partners were scattered around the rim. We were not going to push, but sit until dark to see if we could spot deer feeding on the hillsides.

Reaching the bench, I put Amanda as a hunter and Sue behind a stump and pointed out several places where I thought deer might appear. Telling them I would be right behind them, but out of sight, about 20 yards away, I, too, settled down behind a fallen log and started glassing.

Several minutes passed and I thought I heard deer moving on the far hillside. Glassing, I could not see anything moving, but I knew something was up and moving about, but could not tell where. Thirty or so minutes passed and my wife left Amanda and joined me. Whispering, I told her I thought there were deer moving on the far hillside, but that I could not spot them because they were feeding in the mahogany and snowberry brush.

Sue moved to a better spot to glass. She had just settled into place when off to my right about 200 yards and coming out of a draw were three of the biggest bucks I had seen all season.

Picking up my radio I said urgently, "AMANDA COME HERE NOW!"

She calmly replied, "Where are you?"

"Behind you! Behind you!" I answered frantically.

By the time she arrived, the deer had stopped running and, according to my range finder, were 375 yards away.

They started feeding, and I started getting frustrated. I wanted Amanda to shoot her first buck, but she could not see them.

My frustration also stemmed from the fact, that I could see them in my binoculars, but not in my scope.

My directions to Sue and Amanda only led to further frustration, when they could not see these huge deer standing and feeding on the far hillside.

Finally Amanda excitedly said, "I got them!"

My range finder read 425 yards.

Too far, many of you are thinking; too far for a first-time hunter, but I wanted her to give it a try.

The shooting conditions were perfect. There was no wind, good light, excellent backstop, a tree to use as a rest, and two spotters.

There was no need of asking her if she wanted to shoot. The excitement on her face was my answer. Taking a rest over the log and holding 18 inches over the back of the largest, she slowly squeezed the trigger and missed.

The bucks whirled and headed back toward the draw they had originally come out of, but much higher up the mountain. I whispered to watch the draw because I figured they would cross and head up the far ridge. If they crossed, we would all get a good look at them before they disappeared into the mahogany brush.

Sure enough, within a minute or less, they crossed and headed up the far ridge and stopped and looked around as if to say, "Hmm, I wonder where that shot came from?"

There they stood, three magnificent bucks, 528 yards away, according to my range finder.

"Amanda," I said, "I am going to try a shot if you don't mind."

"Oh, no, go ahead," she answered.

Getting down behind the log, I checked the scale on my scope that I had taped there just after sighting in. It said my 175 grain Barnes X bullet drops 47 inches at 500 yards.

Mentally converting the 47 inches to 4 feet at 528 yards, I held two feet over the two foot high antlers and slowly squeezed the trigger.

There are many who question the sensibility of shooting at such a range and I'll be the first to admit I can debate both sides of the issue. The biggest unknown factor is the ability of the shooter and the knowledge of his rifle. As a former competitor with both handgun and rifle, I will say I used to be able to hold my own in competition and if I did not think I could humanely kill the deer, I would not have fired.

At the shot, the deer disappeared with two of three running for further cover.

Sue, who was glassing excitedly said, "You hit him! He's down!"

"Keep watching," I replied. "I am going up there to see."

With her guiding me in the fading daylight, I was soon scrambling the last few feet to the ridge top.

Immediately I found blood and just off the ridge top was my deer, dead.

It was truly one good shot.

Our campfire session started later that evening, because of the work involved in getting the buck off the hillside, work including gutting, skinning, bagging and finally hanging him in a tree.

There was revelry around the fire, with family and friends smiling and jubilant, asking again and again to hear the story of the hunt. Throwing more wood on the fire, while basking in their praise, it slowly sank in, the realization I would probably never again shoot such a magnificent buck at such a long distance. However, nothing will ever top the adventure or the thrill of the moment when I heard my wife say, "You hit him. He's down."

Next year, when family, friends and longtime hunting partners gather around the campfire on the eve of opening day to share in the excitement of the upcoming hunt, I'll be with them, retelling and reliving the moment I made a perfect shot.

A DOUBLE TAP ON AN ELK

Opening morning of the South Western Oregon Roosevelt elk season, found my son John and me standing in front of a locked gate along with three other members of our hunting party, Rick Spring, Dave Pappel, and Ben Ferguson. The gate was put up to prevent motor vehicles from entering and damaging the rain soaked dirt road system built several years earlier to haul logs out to market.

It had been a "summer show," a logging term that means the roads were only used in the summer when they were dry. Thousands of board feet of timber had been hauled out of King Creek, creating a vast clear-cut, which you have heard me espouse in the past as Mother Nature's breadbaskets for deer and elk.

We knew from previous scouting that there was a herd of 40 cows, four spikes and three branch-antlered bulls feeding and living in the clear-cut. They had been there throughout the warm summer months and into early fall. However, as the fall rains and cold winds of November approached, the elk spent less and less time in the clear-cut and more in the timber where they would have some protection from the elements.

Fortunately, they would come out of the timber and into the clear-cut in the early evening to feed and would often remain until early morning.

Savvy hunters know this is often a good time to harvest the bulls before they headed back into the timber.

If we were lucky this morning, daylight would reveal them to be in the clear-cut, feeding, grazing or dozing, not more than 500 yards beyond our locked gate.

It was the branch antlered bulls we were after. Oregon law requires at least three points on one side to be legal.

We had been counting on having this little hunting area to ourselves.

However, the herd was too big to be considered a secret.

There were three other hunters hanging around the gate, waiting for daylight. Striking up a conversation, we found out they too had been scouting and following this herd for the past six months or so, hoping they would be around for opening day.

There wasn't much sense in getting mad. They had as much right to be there as we did.

Oh sure, I'll admit a little bit of pique entered my mind when I realized our hunting spot was not as protected from others as I thought, but we decided to join forces, at least for the first couple of hours.

Why? So we would not get into each other's way, and to keep the hunt safe.

The herd was there, but we were too late for any shooting. As daylight dawned and it became light enough to see, the herd was on the far side of the clear-cut about 400 yards away and just heading into the timber.

Glassing, it was just light enough to faintly pick out the three big bulls tucked right into the middle of the herd as they slowly meandered out of sight.

One thing in our favor; they were not spooked. They had gone into the timber at a walk, not a dead run. We knew they would not go very far before stopping to lie down and rest.

Quietly assessing our plan with our new friends, John, Rick Spring and I decided we would be the ones to go into the heavy timber after them. We were going to try to do one of two things. The first would be to get in front and hopefully turn the herd, forcing them back out into the clear-cut where the rest of our new hunting party would be waiting. The second, and the reason I opted to go into the woods, would be for us to shoot one or more bulls in the timber.

Over the years, I have not been very successful in turning a herd. I have done it, but I have killed more elk by sneaking up on them in the timber. Getting into position involved a fast truck ride down one mountain and up another. It also involved much hurried walking, almost an hour's worth before we were into position to be out in front of the herd.

John and I normally carry and hunt with Contenders. Usually JD's .375 or .405 Winchester something in a caliber big enough to handle the game we are hunting.

However, because we knew this patch of timber to be full of viney maple, salal, Oregon grape, huckleberry and other bushes, which in order to get through requires some sort of modified low crawl, we decided to take four inch barreled S&W 44 Magnums because they're easier to carry.

Interspersed with the brush were one or two acre-sized areas of ferns and alder, ideal places to find elk. What we intended to do was get through the brush as quietly as we could and catch the elk unaware. It is a lot easier to write about than it is to actually accomplish such a task. We entered the woods agreeing beforehand to split up, with the idea we would go about 400 yards or so down a main ridge and then swing off to the right, pushing toward the clear-cut. We figured that somewhere deep in the woods we would find the elk.

Almost immediately I was silently cursing, as I low crawled through the first patch of huckleberries. I am a big guy with a bad back and crawling does not do much for my lower spine. The only thing that keeps me going is the love of the hunt, and the surge of adrenaline I get when I hear a cow calling for its calf.

Within minutes, I could no longer hear Rick or John but I knew they were in the same sort of mess I was in. Rick probably had it even rougher. He was carrying a long barreled rifle. Oh well, someday he will see the light and ask about hunting with a Contender or some other pistol.

Coming to my first open area, I could see much "sign." Elk beds and fresh tracks were everywhere. The tracks were so fresh I could smell elk. They were close. Deciding to follow a trail they had made, I was soon back on my hands and knees tracking them through the brush.

I do not know how they do it, but elk can push through viney maples as though they did not exist. As I crawled, I heard a cow call its calf. My heart started pounding so fast I was afraid she would hear and whistle alerting the herd to danger.

Lying still with huckleberry bushes framing a canopy over my back, I could hear the chirps and murmurs of feeding elk. The smell and sound of their heavy bodies pushing through the bushes let me know I was so close I was almost afraid I would be stepped on. Slowly I crawled on, hoping I could get to some point where I could stand up and see. If this was the herd we had seen earlier, there had to be some bulls around.

After several minutes of slowly moving, I could see through the bushes and into another opening. The problem was, there was not any way to stand upright without being seen, and spooking the elk.

There were elk all around me in the huckleberries; were some of them bulls?

Eons seemed to pass as I slowly crawled towards the opening. Today, reality tells me it probably was not more than a minute when I could not stand it any longer and I started to slowly get upright in order to see.

What a mistake!

There I am hunched like a man with a broken back, and with huckleberries grabbing at my feet. My head is cocked back, and not more than 20 yards away is the herd cow staring me right in the eye. "OOPS," I thought, "I hope she does not know what I am."

I didn't move, I didn't do anything, but breathe, and I might have even stopped.

With a suspicious look, she broke eye contact and resumed feeding. I took a deep breath and tried to get into a more comfortable position. Trying to adjust my feet and straighten my back at the some time proved to be beyond my physical dexterity, for I promptly and very noisily fell on my ass.

The woods exploded. Elk were going everywhere. Cows were calling, calves were answering, small trees were being bowled over and I was thrashing around trying to stand up.

Getting to my feet, I saw a branch-antlered bull just long enough to draw my 44 and fire. I missed. The herd was running towards my son's position. I started tracking them, hoping he would get a shot.

About ten minutes after my ignominious fall to the forest floor I heard two very quick shots followed by two more. Double taps. I knew it was John because the sound of a pistol is markedly different from a rifle.

Besides, I did not think there was anyone else in the woods with us.

Because there had been four shots, I just knew my son had a bull down.

I moved towards the area where the shots had come from, spotting several cow elk along the way.

Within minutes, I was in the area where I thought he would be and whistled for him. Immediately he whistled back and I could see his orange vest about 100 yards up the hill.

When I got to him he was proudly standing over a 4 point bull that he had killed with two shots from a 4 inch barreled S&W 44 Magnum.

It was a first; no one in our hunting party has ever killed an elk with such a short-barreled handgun.

It seems as though the first two shots were directed at the herd bull, but in his excitement, John missed. As the big bull ran out of sight, the second ran into his sight picture, and he fired another double tap. It ran a few yards and expired.

So what do you do with a 500 pound plus animal you have just killed?

With ducks, geese, pheasants, rabbits and other game animals, you usually pick them up, tuck them into a pack or pocket and walk out. However, it is impossible to pick up a huge elk and carry it to the butcher shop for further processing.

What you do is sit back and assess the situation.

First thing I did was send John out into the clear-cut to get help. Help in this instance meant members of our party going back to the trucks to get packboards, skinning knives, cloth bags, and a tarp.

I stayed behind and tried to gut the elk, but my back was

killing me and it was too big for me to roll over so I just sat back and waited for help to come.

While sitting under a towering Douglas fir tree I started thinking and smiling about John killing an elk with a 4-inch 44 Magnum revolver; a feat I had never accomplished.

My boys as hunters demonstrate students can and do surpass their teacher.

It started raining while John was gone and in a matter of minutes went from a gentle trickle to a full storm. It came down in sheets, the wind started moaning in the treetops and I got cold. Soon my hat was soaked and water started trickling down my back.

My haven under the towering fir became a risky place to be because the wind was tossing huge broken branches about as though they were toothpicks.

As quickly as the wind came, it disappeared, and the rain intensified.

Even though I was wearing rain gear it even found a way to burrow under my jacket and pants until I was soaked and very miserable.

Two guys from the other hunting party showed up, admired John's elk and one with some disappointment in his voice said, "Well good luck getting him out of here, I think we will see if we can get the one you missed."

With that statement, they slowly and quietly moved off into the driving rain.

Time passed and still no John and crew with packboards, knives and stuff. "I wonder what is taking them so long." I had no sooner had this thought when I heard a shout and spied my hunting buddies toiling up through the ferns.

Unfortunately, there was a problem.

The high winds and driving rain had made it difficult for John to communicate what it was he actually needed. The only word my partners could understand was packboards and packboards is all they brought. No rope, no skinning knives, no elk bags, no tarp, no saws, just packboards. I was irked to say the least. After all, we are not amateurs to elk hunting.

They should have known better and brought down everything.

We quickly gutted the elk and decided I, with Ben Ferguson would walk back to the trucks and get the forgotten gear, including lunches.

I took one of the pack frames Dave had brought down, loaded it with every piece of miscellaneous gear the guys were carrying, (binoculars, ammo, pistols, etc.) and headed out.

While I was gone, the remaining three hunters, Rick, John and Dave would skin as much of John's elk as they could with their pocketknives.

It was a long walk out. It took over an hour to get to the rigs and gather up our supplies. By the time, we returned the rain had stopped, but my fellow hunters' lips and finger tips were turning blue from the cold and damp.

While Ben and I were gone, they had skinned half the elk and were ready to do some serious butchering.

I skinned the other hindquarter while they grabbed a quick bite and replenished some fluids. It did not take long with good sharp skinning knives.

The next task was to cut off the hindquarters, put them in clean cloth bags and strap them onto the pack boards. John and Ben were the first to head out each carrying a chunk of meat weighing almost 100 pounds.

I mentioned earlier it took me over an hour to walk out to get our gear. What I did not say was the trip out was almost straight up and extremely difficult because of the mud.

It was the kind of hike where you climb for three to five minutes and then stop to catch your breath. I had enough trouble packing out my body let alone trying it with a tremendous weight on my pack. Of course, I used to do it when I was their age.

Rolling the elk onto the tarp I had brought down, Rick and I made quick work of finishing the skinning. Before John and Ben returned, we had loaded up Tracker Dave with the two front quarters and sent him, slipping, sliding, staggering and yes groaning, on his way.

Five hours had passed since John had completed his double tap on the four point. It was starting to get colder and the rain was back. Conditions were miserable, we were miserable. We were all soaked from rain and physical exertion.

Rick and I decided we would try to get everything out of the woods in one final push when everyone returned. Cutting the ribs off the back strap (spinal column) did not take very long but they were too big to fit into a packframe bag so we lashed them to our pack boards. About the time, we finished tying everything together John and Ben returned. To save time, Ben chose to carry out the entire back strap in one piece. I have no idea how much it weighed, but I know it was well over 125 pounds. It took two of us to pull him to his feet.

John wanted to carry both ribs so we untied one of them, lashing everything together. The only thing we had left to carry out was the head, neck, liver and heart.

The hide and entrails were left behind. Dave returned, picked up the neck and wearily started back out and up on his second trip. Rick and I tied the head to a pack board, packed up all the gear that was left lying around and put it into my packframe. Taking one last look around for any forgotten gear we shouldered our loads and headed out for the long, slippery, exhaustive walk, to the top.

SWAMP DONKEYS AND WHITETAILS

A New Hampshire Hunting Experience

The sound was almost worth fighting over. I was listening to an obnoxiously loud, drawn-out snore followed by the worst sucking, gurgling noises ever to assault my ears and I was trying to sleep. Picture a giant milkshake with just a tad of liquid in the bottom. Toss in a straw and start slurping what's left. The sound would be exactly what I heard as I tossed and turned, trying to figure out how to get away from the noise without having to leave the bunkhouse.

Even though it felt like a nightmare, I was wide awake, far from home in Oregon and back in the family's Northern New Hampshire camp, trying to get to sleep.

In 1951, Dad bought Hurlbert Camp, (still marked as such on the official Fish and Game topographical map) a former logging facility on Crystal Mountain to use as a hunting and fishing retreat. Camp was initially comprised of four buildings; the horse barn, the two story house, cookhouse and bunkhouse. As kids, going to camp became our favorite pastime. While there we would catch brook trout, pick wild raspberries and hunt for partridges and rabbits.

Today, only the cookhouse and bunkhouse remain, a testament to the harsh Northern New Hampshire winters with their annual snowfall of 9 feet or more, that flattened the other two. As a child, camp was a rustic place, and as a older middle-aged adult, it is still rustic, yet a romantic place because of the memories it holds.

There is cold running water from a spring high on the mountain. The bathroom is an outhouse, a one-holer neatly tucked beneath the spruce trees. Light comes from propane or antique kerosene lanterns. Heating and cooking are done with two wood burning stoves. An advantage to growing up in an antique cape in North Central New Hampshire is cooking was and done on a wood-burner (even during summer vegetable canning time). Thus, all of the Sharps' kids are experts in cooking on a wood-burning cook stove.

At camp, I was black powder muzzleloader hunting with my brother, Steve; his son, Jamie; and the guy who snored. His nickname is Jethro Bodine. His real name is Jeff Sawin but he looks and acts like the guy on "The Beverly Hillbillies:" hence, the nickname. At the moment, I did not care who or what he looked and acted like. All I wanted to do was get some sleep.

It was my first time deer hunting with a muzzleloader in New Hampshire, and I was using a .50 caliber Thompson Center Hawken. Steve and I had been planning this four-day trip for more than a year, and now I was so upset from sleep deprivation I was ready to throw Jethro out the bunkhouse door.

It is a long plane ride from Coos Bay, Oregon, to Laconia, New Hampshire, and it is a long truck ride from Laconia north to camp.

Arriving at camp around noon earlier that day, Steve, Jamie and I had hunted deer till dark. Climbing up and around the flanks of Crystal Mountain had so tired me out my body's aches and pains were crying out for sleep.

But Jethro, with his unconscious snoring, had different ideas. The long ride north and the afternoon of hunting in the snowy cold, followed by a steak dinner garnished with mushrooms was enough to insure I would go to bed early.

So I was the first one into the bunkhouse and into bed after dinner. Opening the door, I was greeted by a room so warmly heated by the glowing Jotul stove that I left it open to cool as I climbed into bed, assuming by the time the other guys arrived the place would have cooled off enough to close the door. Unfortunately for me, Jethro and Jamie were right behind, and I swear within two minutes of Jethro's head hitting the pillow, he was snoring.

"Jamie," I asked, "Have you slept in here with Jethro before and is he a snorer?"

"Yes and yes" was his reply. "He gets pretty loud."

"Oh no," I thought silently. As a light sleeper I knew I was in for trouble.

Putting on my portable headset radio, which I had taken to listen to the presidential election returns, I let the automatic search look for a station. I was so far north and so isolated the only thing it could find was a French-speaking radio station out of Quebec. The music was good, catchy, and I whiled away an hour or so trying to remember my high school French as I listened. Every once in awhile, either Jamie or I would yell at Jethro to turn over, and the snoring would cease for a minute or two, just long enough for me to say a quick prayer that I could fall asleep before he started up again.

Around 10, the radio station went off the air; and then, all I heard was the hiss of static and the snores of Jethro. Instead of counting sheep to help me sleep, and with the French music as an incentive I decided to conjugate *"avoir"* and *"etre,"* two French verbs from my high school days. It did not work. I remained awake and Jethro snored on.

I debated getting up and moving in with my brother who, blissfully unaware, was asleep in the cookhouse's double bed. However, we haven't shared a bed since we were little kids, and at my age, I did not want to start again. I kept thinking if I harassed Jethro enough, he would quit.

He didn't.

At midnight I got up, dressed, and went for a walk down the camp's access road, but it was so cold I quickly returned with the resolve to put an end to the snoring.

Returning to the bunkhouse, I pleaded with Jethro to turn over and try to quit snoring. Obviously he sleeps flat on his back, mouth wide open, without a care in the world or he wouldn't make so much noise. He mumbled something about he would and kept right on snoring. Desperate, I picked up a glass filled with cold water and poured it into his open mouth. Choking and sputtering he never became fully conscious but sat up, half-turned, flopped around, and fell back onto his back, still snoring. So I grabbed him by the seat of his underwear and back of his shirt and literally forced him over onto his stomach. He stopped snoring. Ahhh! Mission accomplished.

As I slid under the covers, of my bed, I heard Jamie laughing (and Jethro starting to snore again). Sometime between midnight and 3, I know I fell asleep, but I was awakened at 3 a.m. by a particularly loud snore and gurgles. I silently cursed the man who was making my lifetime hunt so miserable.

Jethro's alarm went off at 4:30, and he let it ring until the tension was gone out of the spring before it was silent. I knew he was awake because he wasn't snoring, just yawning like a tired guy needing his sleep. He had to get up because he had volunteered to cook breakfast, which meant Jamie, and I could stay in bed for another hour.

Later, as I entered the cookhouse, I was greeted by my brother, who, with a knowing smile, inquired, "So how did you sleep?"

"Pretty good," I replied. "But I've slept better."

"Well, Jethro says you and Jamie yelled at him all night long and he didn't sleep a wink."

"He slept," I replied smilingly. "But, undoubtedly, he has experienced quieter nights."

No more was said about sleeping until later that evening.

Over breakfast, we planned and refined our hunt. Breakfast was bacon, eggs, and Mom's English muffins slathered in homemade strawberry jam. There was also hot tea for me, and coffee for the rest of the guys.

We decided to work our way to the top of Crystal Mountain, where deer are known to cross if other hunters push them. Jamie and Jethro would hunt together, staying behind, and to the right, of Steve and me, in order to ambush any deer we might jump out of their beds on our way to the top. They knew deer always break or run right on this side of the mountain.

It would take us about three hours to work through our hunt plan and regroup on the top, because it was over a mile to the top.

At daylight, as we left the warmth and comfort of the cook shack, we stepped outside into cold, crisp New Hampshire weather.

From all indications, it was going to be a bright, sunny day, though snow was forecast for the evening. I was like a little kid, excited about the prospect of watching it snow because it does not snow where I live.

Steve, Jamie and Jethro were wearing their "woolies", heavy wool pants and jackets and insulated boots. As for me, I had on my typical Oregon hunting clothes of wranglers, hickory shirt, and heavy wool sweater for the New Hampshire cold, Browning's leather hunting boots, Cabela's Gortex raingear, mittens and a borrowed orange fluorescent cap, and lastly, my battered and well-worn orange vest that I have owned and hunted in for many years and won't give up.

Steve and I wished the others good luck and slowly started our way up the mountain. Carrying my late father's .50 caliber Thompson Center Hawken loaded with a maxi-ball only added to the excitement. Knowing our prospects were good, I felt that I might, just might, shoot my first whitetail deer. Soon, by choice, Steve and I were separated by a hundred yards or more. Occasionally, off to my left, I could spot his orange hat or hear the snow crunch under his boots.

Steve, who had killed a 224-pound, eight-point buck on opening day, was acting, as my guide and was not carrying a rifle. However, he was armed with a Fox Sterlingworth 20-gauge shotgun and was hunting partridges. Partridge hunting is as important to Steve as hunting deer.

Less than 10 minutes from camp, I was startled to hear a muzzleloader fire off to my right. "Wow!" I thought, "That was quick." I assumed either Jamie or Jethro had spotted and shot at a deer. Jamie was carrying a .50 caliber Hawken identical to mine, and Jethro had a scope-sighted 50-caliber, in-line from Gonic arms.

I stood silently, hoping that if they had missed the deer, it would come my way. Minutes passed and there were no more shots or any yells for help. We had earlier agreed if someone downed a deer, they would let others know to come and help.

Steve came my way and we agreed, while whispering, that obviously someone had missed and we might as well continue on our way to the top.

It was a beautiful walk. Deer and "swamp donkey" sign was everywhere. "Swamp donkeys" is an affectionate term originally used by Jethro whenever he discusses moose. It is one I liked and adopted, because they do look like huge donkeys as they stride, run or gallop through the woods. Before my trip was over, I was to see 11 swamp donkeys; two were huge bulls, so close I could have hit them with a snowball.

By 10 o'clock, my coat was open, my mittens were off and I had stuffed my hat into a pocket in an attempt to cool down. No doubt, I was moving too fast as I made my way up the mountain, but the warming temperatures and the rising sun were affecting my body temperature.

Stopping for a break beneath an old tree stand erected by our deceased brother, Ed, Steve and I sadly reminisced about how he and our late father had loved this mountain and about how many deer they had killed on its flanks. We were following in their footsteps, using the same game trails and paths blazed by them when they first hunted on Crystal Mountain years ago. We stood awhile silently, cherishing memories.

We separated again, but not before Steve reminded me swamp donkeys were apt to be found in a flat that I would soon be crossing.

It was the legs that first caught my eye: long, black, angular-looking things that did not match the surrounding trees. My heart started beating quickly because I knew a swamp donkey was just yards away. Stopping to glass, I finally figured out a cow moose and calf were standing looking toward Steve. Slowly I inched my way forward until I could see them without any brush obstructing my view. Trying to get into a better position I stepped on something, which cracked, and they were gone in their familiar rocking, galloping lope. Already made suspicious by Steve's presence, they were not about to stick around to find out what spooked them.

Minutes later, Steve came by and with a huge grin asked, "Did you see the moose?"

"Yes," I replied excitedly, and once again we started reminiscing about camp and the way it had been when we were kids.

Moose were almost unheard of in the early' 50s.

As time and years passed, they became so abundant a hunting season was established. One fall day, while hunting partridges, Steve had met an enraged bull during rut and had to take refuge in a tree. On another occasion, Edward had been stalked and finally charged by a moose that left him alone when he started firing warning shots over its back.

Around 11:30 or so, Steve and I reached the top of Crystal Mountain. We had expected Jamie and Jethro to be waiting, because they had had an easier trek, but repeated whistling brought no response, so we decided to eat lunch. I rested my rifle against a stump and picked still another further away for a seat. As we quietly chatted and munched on wonder bars, I noticed Steve's eyes grow wide and heard him exclaim, in a whisper "Buck! Buck! There is a huge buck over there."

My back was to the deer, my rifle was about four feet away, and by the time I had everything put together, the deer was gone. Grabbing my rifle, I ran down a game trail, meandering through some low-growing spruce trees, hoping for a glimpse of the buck if he were to run by the backside of the ridge we were on.

My pounding heart and gasps for air convinced me my run was futile as I reluctantly gave up the chase. Returning back along the path, I met Steve carrying my jacket, vest, hat, mittens and the rest of the clothes I had discarded as we had sat in the sun.

As we discussed Steve's sighting, he said the buck literally ran out of the woods into the clearcut where we rested as though it was being pursued by someone or some thing. We learned later that Jamie and Jethro had tired of waiting for us and that they had been tracking the buck Jamie had fired at and missed earlier that day. Unbeknownst to us, Jethro had been tracking the buck Steve saw and it was following a game trail out of the woods, hightailing away from him.

This was all learned later. Steve told me to get on a stand where he thought the deer might cross, and he would track it, hoping I would get a shot.

As I made my way to the stand, I was almost startled out of my boots as a huge bull moose rocketed up out of its bed and raced away down the mountain. My heart was beating so fast, I had to stop and rest awhile. Within 30 minutes or so, Steve arrived, once again asking if I had seen the moose, and we discussed how we were going to find the buck he had seen earlier.

Crystal Mountain is long and narrow, running east to west with three tops. We were on the official top but still had a mile or more of ridge to follow before we would have to drop off the left flank to make our way back to camp. We decided to separate and follow the ridge top to see if we could jump another deer out of its bed. Probably an hour or more passed when we ran into Jamie, but not Jethro.

Jamie told us he had been the one who fired earlier in the morning. Evidently on our way up the mountain, Steve and I had jumped it from its bed. He had missed, and they had been tracking it for most of the day. He told us they had found Steve's track when he had tried to push it to my position. Because they knew we were in the area, Jethro made a wide loop down off the east side of Crystal Mountain trying to get closer to the buck and to again pick up its tracks.

After listening to Jamie, and because he knows the mountain so well, Steve was able to instantly assess the situation and knew how to modify the hunting plan to our advantage and to benefit Jethro's stalking.

As we made our way to a new stand, we heard branches and limbs cracking just ahead, "Moose," said Steve.

Peering through the trees, I could see two black animals standing looking back over their shoulders trying to figure out what had disturbed their afternoon nap.

Bulls and one was huge. As I fumbled in my coat pocket, trying to get my camera, they bolted. Their antlers slapped and cracked against the trees as they, with their now familiar rocking gait, bolted out of sight.

"This is the spot where I want you guys to wait," said Steve. "Deer cross here as well as moose." "Jamie,' he said. "I want you to get to Charlie's right about 100 yards and sit quietly. I'll be back in an hour or so and between Jethro and me, we ought to push a deer through here."

Sitting quietly for me is pure agony. I detest it. In Oregon, I am the guy who pushes deer to those who wait. I find it almost impossible to sit still for more than a minute, and now I was expected to sit for an hour or more?

I tried, and for the most part, I was successful. Stamping out a place in the snow for my feet so they would not get too cold, I also brushed snow off a stump for a semi-dry place to sit. My view was great and I just knew Steve or Jethro would push a deer our way.

As I sat, seconds turned to minutes, minutes to an hour.

I swear my watch stopped on several occasions. As the sun sunk lower in the sky, passing below the ridgeline, the air became colder and I started to shiver. The wind came up and its low moan through the treetops was spooky, only adding to my misery and shivering. My feet encased in my allegedly waterproof Gortex Browning boots felt damp and my toes were numb. During the hour or more that I sat, I put on my mittens and hat, which I had removed while walking in the sun; zipped up my coat and huddled deeply inside, trying to stay warm.

Still no Steve or Jethro.

Finally, I could not stand it any longer. I started to get up and move around in order to get warm, when I heard a loud "woof" off to my right where Jamie was sitting. Instantly I became warm as adrenalin surged throughout my body, all thoughts of being cold were gone. I recognized the sound a deer makes clearing its nostrils of the hated scent of man.

Slowly lifting my Hawken to the ready position, I waited for the deer to pass below me.

"Kaboom!" roared a muzzleloader off to my right.

Several minutes passed and I slowly made my way over to Jamie. "Did you get him?" I asked.

"I don't know," replied Jamie. "I fired at a huge buck running up that trail," he said, pointing off and down to our left about 80 yards away. "After I fired, he whirled and ran."

"Well, let me go see if I can find some blood or hair indicating a wound."

Making my way down the hill, I soon discovered tracks of a running deer in the snow. Several minutes later I found a huge patch of blood in the snow. "You hit him," I hollered. "Come on down and let's start tracking him."

"Hey," Said a voice from further up the ridge.

"Who's there?" I replied.

"Jeff," (Jethro) came the answer. "Did you get him? I have been tracking that guy all day."

"No," I answered, "But we have blood."

Soon Jamie, Steve and Jethro joined me, and we started the painstaking task of tracking a wounded deer. Within minutes, the blood spots became the size of a dime and eventually they ceased. From the evidence of blood found up on the ferns, it appeared that Jamie's non-fatal shot hit the buck high on the outside of its right shoulder as it was running straight toward him when he fired.

As we tracked the deer farther down off the mountain and farther away from camp, the snow disappeared. The deer was moving fast, and it was obvious we were not going to catch him before dark.

Reluctantly, we gave up the chase and made the long haul back up Crystal Mountain and down the other side toward camp. As I stumbled along in my wet feet, I played and replayed the shooting in my mind, trying to figure out if we could have done something differently, while wondering if we should go back in the morning and look for the deer.

I was startled out of my reverie as three swamp donkeys; their heads head high, bolted for safety. If you could see them, taller at the shoulder than the haunch, running with their rocking gait, you would really understand the nickname.

They were spooky because moose-hunting season had finished the Wednesday before I arrived and, without a doubt they were expecting a shot or two to be launched their way.

Reaching camp about an hour before dark, I'll admit I was tired. No, exhausted would be a better term, from all the tramping around I had done. My feet were sore, my boots even though new, were ruined. The rubber soles were cut to shreds from the rough ground I had been trodding upon for the past two days. My legs and hips ached and all I wanted was a hot shower and some dry clothes. The hot shower was out of the question, but dry socks and pants and a shot of apricot brandy while snuggled up next to the stove soon had me feeling better.

Steve and Jethro wanted to try one more hunt down off the mountain near a spruce bog; I opted not to go and went to the bunkhouse to catch up on my sleep. I must have dozed an hour or so (after all Jethro was out hunting) when Steve burst through the door exclaiming, "Jethro killed a doe!"

He had come back to camp to get rope, a camera, and help to drag the deer back up the hill.

New Hampshire requires that all deer killed have to be checked by an authorized fish and game station within 12 hours of being slain. Checking involves weighing, recording the type of weapon used, verifying hunting license, home address, location of kill, etc. The nearest checking station from camp is in the town of Pittsburg, about two hours from camp. After getting the doe back to camp, we elected to have supper before Steve and Jethro headed to town. I already figured I'd skip town, get to bed early and would be asleep when they returned.

Jethro's snoring was not going to bother me that night.

Supper was more mashed potatoes, deer tenderloin, vegetables and tea or coffee with a rehash of the day's hunt. Around 7:30, discussion lagged because we were tired, so Steve and Jethro decided they should get to town before the checking station closed. As they were leaving, I said, "Good hunting Jethro, but I'm tired and off to bed."

The bunkhouse was way too warm for comfortable sleeping, so I opened the door and window as wide as they could go and crawled into my sleeping bag knowing, I would soon be, "dead to the world," dreaming of the big buck I would shoot on the morrow.

It just wasn't in the cards.

It seems as though I had just gotten asleep when I heard the guys returning from town. There was some commotion as they hung the doe high in a tree because they were having difficulty getting the gambrel through her back legs.

Soon Jethro came into the bunkhouse, mumbling something about the place being as cold as a barn, closed the door and window, and climbed into bed.

Within minutes came his horrible gurgling snore, the one I had learned to hate the night before.

"Jethro," I remarked. "Either you turn over or I swear you'll be sleeping outside tonight."

"Okay, okay," he mumbled as he rolled over and stopped snoring.

No doubt it was because I was so tired his snoring let me sleep fitfully until 3 a.m. or so. After a particularly loud snort, which had awakened me, I thought I could hear the old familiar hiss of snow hitting the treetops, which are all around the cabin. Deciding to get up to go to the bathroom and to satisfy my curiosity, I opened the door to an entirely new, beautiful and mystical world. A world of white driving snow coming down so fast and furiously it almost obscured the cookhouse 50 feet away.

I knew it would be almost impossible to find the deer Jamie had shot the day before. The storm would also cause the deer to take cover and wait it out in spruce and balsam thickets. Hunting would be slower in the morning, the tracking enhanced; it would be good day hunting.

Loading the stove full of wood, I returned to bed to listen to Jethro's gurgling concerto and waited for dawn.

There was no hurry for us to get up because it was snowing hard and we all knew chances of bagging a deer would be slim.

However, we were all deer hunters and knew it was possible to jump deer out of their snug beds if they were pushed, and tracking would be excellent.

We were ready to hunt just after daylight.

We entered the woods behind the bunkhouse, circling about a quarter-mile in diameter. We were somewhat scattered; our main task was to look for fresh deer tracks and then when they were found, to give pursuit. About 20 minutes into the circle, Steve gave a sharp whistle to get my attention and when I found him, he silently pointed at the ground. I knew he had fresh deer sign.

The rest of the morning was spent unsuccessfully tracking deer, spending interminable hours at stands, hoping something or someone would come by. It continued to snow and the low pressure of the storm insured deer would remain ensconced in some warm and protected haven.

Early in the afternoon, when I thought I could not stand the cold any longer, even though my toes were snug and warm in my borrowed boots, I heard a familiar whooping call from my brother which meant, "Meet me back at the cookhouse. It's time for a late lunch."

After lunch, it continued to snow, and we unsuccessfully tramped around looking for deer and deer sign before returning to camp around 4.

Some of the best news I had heard on the trip came when we returned to camp. Jethro was leaving, going home and not returning while I was at camp. It was a gift; I was not going to have to listen to him snore. I even helped Jethro take his deer down and put it into his truck, just in case he thought he should stick around to help us fill our tags. The one thing I didn't do was pack his duffle bag or strip his bunk, although the thought crossed my mind.

While outside waving goodbye, tears came to my eyes, not from sadness because Jethro was leaving, but from the cold wind and snow stinging my cheeks.

The next morning after a peaceful night's sleep, I found it had stopped snowing. The weather was gray, overcast and according to earlier news reports, which I had previewed at home, it was apt to start snowing again that afternoon.

There was no question about how we would hunt. After a day of being snuggled someplace out of the weather, deer were going to be hungry. Any tracks we found were going to be fresh and worth following.

Immediately after leaving camp, we discovered fresh tracks out behind the bunkhouse. However, they were not very productive as we tracked and or circled ahead trying to get close enough to spot deer. Several hours went by and we decided to go elsewhere to look.

Elsewhere, in this case, was down by some old beaver ponds and a swamp where we used to fish for trout when we were kids. An old logging trail runs along side the beaver ponds and in the valley between Crystal and Cedar Mountains. It was on that road we hoped to find a fresh buck track.

Around noon, we found a nice set of buck tracks leading across the road and into the swamp. The tracks were big enough and fresh enough to follow. We made plans for Jamie and me to go part way up Cedar Mountain, while Steve tracked the buck.

Hopefully, the buck learning it was being tracked, would allow itself to be pushed up into a crossing Steve knew about. Jamie and

I would be waiting at the crossing and if all worked the way we planned, one of us should get a shot.

The only problem with the plan was I did not go where Steve told us to go. Oh, sure; I followed his directions, spooking an old moose up out of his bed in the process. But Steve intended we only go several hundred yards up Cedar Mountain and sit where we could look into the swamp. I didn't know the country and went where I thought deer might cross, which was about 500 yards farther up the mountain on an old logging road. Logging roads allow excellent visibility, particularly as a deer crossing. It was a fairly decent road and as Jamie and I got into position, I wondered why Steve had not mentioned it as a reference point for me to follow.

About 45 minutes after getting into position I felt I should move. Moving meant going down the road about 100 yards, which would put me closer to Jamie and would, I hoped, give me a better view if a buck should cross the road..

As I eased into my new position I glassed for Jamie and spotted him about 75 yards to my right front, high on a knob, overlooking the road. As I watched, he stiffened and acted as though he could see something. At the same time, I heard a loud crack in the direction he was looking. Glassing, I could see a huge set of antlers bobbing up and down in the brush as a buck casually made his way across the road.

Heart tripping at a hundred miles per hour, I raised my rifle and waited for him to cross into a clearing for a shot.

"KA-boom!" Jamie fired.

I started running down the road to where I had seen the buck.

"Did you get him?" I hollered.

"I'm not sure; I think I had a good shot but he ran away after I fired."

"Okay," I replied. "You stay there and guide me to the place he was standing when you fired."

Within seconds, I was standing on the spot and could see huge tracks running off up the side of Cedar Mountain.

"I have his tracks," I told Jamie. "Sit tight and I'll go see if I can find some blood."

Tracking, I covered 25, 50, and 75 yards, with no signs of a hit. Roughly 100 yards from where I started tracking, I found huge blotches of blood. The snow for several feet around was stained bright red.

"You hit him! "I yelled." "I have lots of blood."

Jamie made his way over and we decided I would start tracking while Jamie went after Steve.

Tracking a bleeding deer in the snow is simple. The only problem was this deer kept on going. Every second I expected to see him lying dead just ahead, but all I saw was tracks leading me farther up the mountain.

I found a huge patch of blood where he had actually fallen over before struggling back onto his feet. Slowly the tracks circled until they were headed back down the mountain toward the swamp. About then I could hear Steve and Jamie whistling trying to find out how far ahead of them I was as they followed my tracks.

The first thing Steve said when he caught up to me was, "What in the heck are you guys doing way up here on top of the mountain? You were supposed to be a quarter of a mile of more in that direction," he said as he pointed downhill.

"What's it matter?" was my quick retort. "We saw, and Jamie fired at a buck."

"You're right," he replied with a grin. "Let's go find this deer."

We split up. Steve went to my right and Jamie to the left. I stayed on the deer's trail. Within minutes I heard Jamie say, "I see him."

"KAboom!" He fired.

"He's going! He's still running!" he yelled excitedly.

As Jamie reloaded, I took off at a dead run, trying to catch a deer so full of adrenalin it did not know it was supposed to be dead.

Leaving Jamie and Steve behind, I soon spotted a huge buck standing behind a log looking at me. Raising my TC Hawken I aimed just behind his shoulder and pulled the trigger. Click, A misfire. I tried again. Click, another misfire.

Looking like he was going to bolt, I tried a third time. "KAboom!" My gun fired and Jamie's buck collapsed.

Frantically I tried to reload but could not get my ramrod out from under the barrel. It was swollen from being constantly wet and I was desperate. The buck was struggling to get to his feet and I knew it was going to run.

"Where is Jamie?" I thought, "He needs to shoot it again before it runs away."

By then, Jamie was right behind me as the buck took off running, with Jamie right behind.

Steve stopped and helped me get my ramrod out and I hastily reloaded.

"KAboom!" I heard Jamie fire again.

"He's down! He's down!" he hollered.

"About time," I replied. "He was one tough deer."

Walking over to Jamie and his deer, I thought about how tenacious this buck was. We later discovered he had four maxi balls in his chest cavity, any one of which should have killed him.

We took pictures of the valiant buck and of each other posing with it. It was a combined effort that we will remember. Steve told Jamie he would pay to have the head mounted in memory of one of the finest hunts we had ever been on and, more importantly, the largest buck Jamie had ever killed.

Steve and I argued about the correct way to remove his entrails. Believe it or not there are some subtle differences between those of us who gut deer on the West Coast versus those on the east.

Steve won the argument and I let him gut the deer.

Then we started the long haul back to camp. It was about a mile and half drag back, most of it uphill. Initially we started downhill and I was in my element. After all, anyone can drag a 226.5-pound deer on snow, downhill. Unfortunately, we hit the swamp within 100 yards, and it took awhile to get him through the tangle of mud, snow, running water, willow whips, and low growing spruce.

Steve and I alternated pulling on one side. We would pull until our lungs and legs wouldn't let us pull anymore. Jamie, a tough young logger, never did get to take a break. As a rest from the pulling, Steve or I would carry the two rifles and shotgun about 50 yards or so and then wait until the other reached the gun stash. Then we would switch and the other guy would carry the firearms up the trail.

Fortunately, we had an ace in the hole by the way of camp's old jeep. When we got within a quarter-mile of camp, we were able to get to the buck with it and saved ourselves about an hour of backbreaking work.

We took the deer to town to the checking station, where we found it was the second-largest muzzle-loading whitetail checked in that year. Word quickly spread around town that there was a large buck at the checking station, and other hunters as well as townspeople came to see it and to congratulate Jamie.

Returning to camp was uneventful; it had stopped snowing, the stars were out; and we were all looked forward to a good night's sleep.

We left camp the next day, but not before sawing down a large spruce, which threatened to lean onto the bunkhouse. While buttoning up camp and replacing the year-round bear-proof shutters over the windows, I silently told myself, "If it is possible, I want my sons, John and Joe, to be with me next fall to hunt whitetail deer. They should have the opportunity to develop memories by seeing swamp donkeys while hunting whitetails in the northern woods of New Hampshire.

UNDER THE BARN WITH
AN UNLAWFUL ELK

Elk hunting is hard work. Fortunately, it is also one of the most exhilarating of all big game hunts. The animals are huge and in Oregon, in hunting areas, they must have at least three points on one side of their racks to be considered legal for hunting.

This particular hunt started like all the rest of ours, by meeting for breakfast in a local café to decide the exact particulars of where my hunting party was going to hunt.

The area is usually decided before we meet, but vagaries of nature such as rain, fog and sleet, sometimes can force us to reconsider.

Oregon hunting regulations not only require three point bulls to be legal, they also require hunters to choose which season they are going to hunt. The first is usually one weekend followed by three weekdays, ending on Wednesday evening.

Second season is two weekends with the five weekdays in the middle.

Many individuals, including our party consider first season to be the best. The elk have not been hunted and they are less spooky insuring a higher success rate for hunters.

However, my hunting party of six has killed as many elk during second season as first, so we really don't have any proof that earlier is better. We just think it is better.

In order to keep hunting fair, we take turns applying for second-and-first season tags. First and second seasons are usually under-subscribed, so there is never a problem getting the tag one applies for.

To make things even more interesting, some of us apply for and receive special elk tags. Black powder and or handgun hunting are several of my favorites. This year I had a black powder tag. Two of my hunting buddies had first-season tags and the other three had second-season tags.

Opening morning found us at our usual café (Mom's), eating hashbrowns and scrambled eggs with minced ham.

Taking a count of who had what tag, we discovered there was only one first- season tag among the five of us. The sixth partner had to work and was unable to make opening morning.

During scouting, we had discovered a herd that had seven branched-antlered bulls running with 40 or so cows and spikes.

Oregon law allows non-tag holders to hunt with tag holders, as long as they do not carry firearms. Non-hunters go along to dog, or to help drive elk to shooting stands. More importantly, they are along to help when the backbreaking chore of removing an elk from the forest begins.

One elk meant six of the seven bulls we had located would probably be around for the rest of the guys for second season.

During the planning at Mom's, it was agreed the tag holder Dave, would go into a fringe of timber where we hoped he would find elk bedded on the edge of a clear cut. He would go with two other hunters tagging along, and with my son John, I would get into a blocking position so we could try and turn the herd if they spooked before one was killed.

Sitting high above the clear cut on a tree-covered, wind-swept ridge, waiting for the sun to rise, I could hear the ocean pounding against the shore and the deep-throated moan of the fog horn warning ships rocks were about and to be on guard.

"Sort of makes you glad you live here, doesn't it, son?" I remarked, as we shivered in the early morning chill waiting for the sound of a gunshot.

"Boom!" The .338 Winchester we had been waiting for roared

down in the valley. "Whump!" The sound of a bullet striking flesh echoed back up to our ridge top.

Minutes passed and the rifle boomed again, and again we heard the sound of a bullet striking flesh.

"He must have wounded it on the first shot," I said.

"Yea," remarked John. "He tends to get excited when big bulls are around."

"We should wait five or 10 minutes for the herd to get up here, but I think he's got his elk."

"Sure sounded like it," he replied.

Soon we heard sticks snapping, branches cracking and elk calves mewling for their mothers. A herd of cows, calves and bulls passed within feet of us, following as we knew they would, a trail they had been using all summer. A trail that would lead them into the safety of the deep woods.

"Did you notice how many bulls were in the herd?" I asked.

"I only saw five," my son said, "but I could have missed one in the timber."

"I hope so," I silently remarked.

The two shots, both with sounds of strikes, had me spooked.

As we turned to go, I heard my distant hunting partner give a yell of jubilation.

"Sounds like he got one, Dad. Let's go help him."

We climbed back up to the ridge top and hiked over to our truck.

We had to drive about two miles of gravel road to get into a position where we could glass the area where the shots had come from.

"I see him," said my son John. "He's gutting a bull on the ridge above the bear bowl."

"Oh, yea!" I remarked. "Man! That's a big one."

Hopping back into the truck, we continued to drive down a gravel road we knew would take us within winching distance of our partner's elk.

As we approached the hunter, my son said, "Oh damn! Dad, look at that."

That was a seven-point bull lying dead on the hillside about 100 yards below and around the hillside from our shooting partner.

I started feeling sick. Instantly I knew what had happened. The first shot had been a mortal one. The shooter, excited, anxious and no doubt nervous had thought he had missed. Seeing his elk walk off, in the low light of early morning and not knowing he had already killed a bull, he put his sights on another and pulled the trigger.

Two shots, two elk. Unfortunately, we had only one tag, Dave's.

Hiking up to the hunters, Rick, Ben, and Dave, who were busy gutting their elk, I could not help myself and said, "Why in hell did you shoot two?"

"What the **#** are you talking about?" was Dave's response.

"There is another dead elk lying just down the ridge from this one," I said.

"We are the only ones hunting out here; you are the only one with a rifle. We heard you fire two shots. Who in hell else would have killed it?"

I was angry and scared. Shooting an extra elk is as against the law here in Oregon as it is in the rest of the country.

Soon all five hunters were gathered around debating what should be done. Suggestions were made, and they ran the gamut of calling the Fish and Wildlife and turning ourselves in, to wasting a beautiful game animal by leaving it out for the coyotes, or going to town and get a hunter who had a legal tag.

Together, we agreed. Someone would go to town and get a tag.

Meanwhile, the five of us wrestled the gutted bull with its legal tag affixed to its ear down the ridge and into the back of a pickup.

Once it was loaded, Rick headed for town to rustle up another tag. Ben went to gut the untagged elk lying on the hillside, while the rest of us headed to a hanging tree to get the hide off the legal bull.

Driving to the hanging tree, I remarked to my son, "We are really stupid. All it would take to get busted would be for a game warden to come driving down the logging road and spot the elk lying on the hillside and we would really have to pay."

"Well," said John, "If we turn in the shooter, he's going to have to pay. Is that fair?"

"No," I answered, "But life is not fair and I am not sure we could ever convince anyone it was not intentional."

It did not take too long to get the hide off the first elk, quarter it and put back into a pickup. As we worked, we speculated by that the time we finished with the elk that our first hunting partner would have returned with another hunter and tag.

No such luck.

We decided we would all go back to the first elk and load it into my truck and start taking the hide off.

"Just what I need," I thought. "A huge, illegal bull in the bed of my truck. How in hell would I explain that to my wife, family, boss and community?"

With a lot of work, rapidly beating hearts and fear, we loaded the elk, which was so huge its feet and head hung over the side, and headed back to the top of the ridge and toward our hanging tree.

The first elk was sent into town with John, Ben and Dave to be put into our walk-in cooler. I suggested to John, that someone get on the citizen's band radio and try and find out what was going on regarding another tag.

I was feeling sick. I was angry at myself for jeopardizing my son's hunting rights and the kind of message we all were giving to the younger hunters.

We were all in an untenable position.

In my mind, things were not getting better. They were getting worse.

As I drove to the top, alone with my illegal elk, the CB squawked and I heard Rick say, "Hey Charlie, I cannot find the guy you sent me looking for. But I have an idea."

He suggested I meet him at a vacant barn, where we could hang and skin the elk privately until my son returned with a tag.

"In for a penny in for a pound,' I was thinking. I could have argued I was taking the elk into town to the game warden for disposal, but that argument would not hold water if we were discovered with an elk in a barn.

The kicker to agreeing was I knew the location. It was just off the property we were hunting. It was at the end of a long gravel road, and best of all, it was behind two locked gates.

I was starting to feel better. There had to be at least one guy in town who would be willing to tag an elk he had not shot. I also thought it was a good idea providing we could get into the barn unseen.

Twenty minutes later, I backed into a huge barn and closed the door.

"Man, I hope those guys get back here soon. I am tired of being spooked," I said to no one in particular.

The barn was long and filled with farming implements. Turning on the lights, we figured the best place to hang the elk would be at the far end underneath the wooden ramp which leads to the upper hay storage portion of the barn.

I threw a heavy rope which we had tied to a gambrel, over the beam. The gambrel was between the elk's hind legs. Tying the free end of the rope to my truck's trailer hitch, I slowly dragged the elk out of the truck and up into the air. He was so long his head and neck was still on the ground.

Several hours had passed. Maybe I could relax. Fear and anger had given me cotton mouth. I decided it was time to take a break. Popping the tab of a Pepsi and taking a deep gulp, I sat down and thought, "Let the younger guys do the skinning. After all, it is just minutes to town and they ought to be back any minute."

Minutes passed and no one came back from town. Talking quietly with Rick, we decided that the hide was not going to come off by itself and we might as well get to work.

Earlier we had cut the feet off. So it did not take very long before I was punching and pulling the hide down around the middle of the back. As we worked, we speculated as to why it was taking the other guys so long to get back from town.

Stopping to sharpen my knife, I thought I heard a voice.

"Shh," I said. "Did you hear someone talking?"

"Are you nuts?" replied Rick. "This is private property and we have the only key to the gates. The only way anyone could get in here would be to walk and then they would be trespassing."

"Well I know I am spooky, but I'd swear I heard men's voices."

"Naah," was his response.

"Oh, damn!" I whispered and pointed.

Through the cobweb covered windows I could see a jeans-covered leg.

Slowly, the leg moved toward the east end of the barn, headed around to the ramp.

The ramp I was hiding under with an illegal elk. The ramp that was warped, rotten, and so full of holes one had to pick their way across the boards to keep from falling through.

I could tell from the voices they were discussing an old car parked on the barn floor. It was apparent one man was trying to sell the car to the other.

Crouching down behind the elk I watched the guys pick there way over my head and into the barn.

"Whew!" I thought. "How could they have missed me?"

Hollow footsteps echoed into the interior where we were hiding.

To this day, I do not know which was louder; their footsteps or the pounding of my heart.

Slowly, I walked the length of the floor and turned off the lights and the truck's CB, fully expecting someone to holler, "Who's down there?"

Whispering, we finally figured out the former renter had returned to sell a car he had left behind to the guy he had brought with him. It was obvious they had walked in because we had not heard the sound of their vehicle.

"Oh, man!" I thought. "Whatever is keeping the other guys from coming back; I hope it keeps them for another hour or so."

Twenty long minutes passed and the voices would rise and fall following the arguing of what was a fair sum for the car. Twenty minutes when I again damned myself for getting into the position I was in. Twenty minutes which seemed like twenty hours while we sat quietly in the barn listening and wondering when they would decide to come downstairs to look at the farm implements which were also mentioned as being for sale.

"Not interested," were probably the sweetest words I heard that day. "I just want this car."

Once again, footsteps picked their way down the rotten old ramp and the jeans-clad leg passed in front of the window. Five more minutes went by and in the far distance; I heard a truck start and the sound of its motor fade off as it drove away.

Slowly, my partner and I started to relax and breathe normally.

"Man, we were lucky," said Rick.

"I wonder what's keeping the other guys?" I asked.

Returning to the truck, I turned on the CB to hear my son calling.

"What have you been doing?" he asked. I have been calling for 20 minutes."

"You will never believe me if I tell you," I replied. "I'll wait until you get here and then explain."

They soon unlocked two gates and drove the several hundred yards to the barn. As they drove up, Ben, with a big grin, waved the long-waited for tag out the window.

A quick head count showed that the original party of five was all in attendance. "Where in hell did they get the tag?"

"Where's Jack (the guy they had gone looking for) and how did you get his tag?"

"His wife says he's hunting up Big Creek," responded a partner. "The reason we took so long was because we had to find another tag."

"Where did you get this one?" I asked.

"Yesterday, Grady told me he was going to go to the Oregon/ Washington football game. That is why he's not hunting with us today. I went to his house and borrowed it," answered John.

At that point the entire group who had gone to town started laughing.

"What in hell is so funny?" I exploded. "We have waited hours for you guys to get back. Rick and I have been stuck under this damn barn with an illegal elk, while two guys snooped around overhead...cops could have been here at any time; and you think it is funny?"

"Hey Dad, lighten up," said John. "We have a tag. Show me the elk and let's make it legal and I will tell you why we laughed."

As he attached the tag to the ear of the elk, he went on to explain no one was home at Grady's.

Normally Grady's house is unlocked and his buddies, including my sons, go in and out as though it were Grand Central Station.

But it was locked and knowing I was desperate for a tag, they applied a little Yankee ingenuity and crawled through the fireplace firewood hole. The humor was the hole was stacked with firewood and had to be removed before one of them could crawl through. They made a mess on the carpet with sawdust and wood chips and had to stop to vacuum. They knew I'd be upset because it was taking longer than planned, but wanted to leave things as they had found them.

They found the tag on his dresser where Grady had shown it to them yesterday when he was bemoaning the fact he could not go hunting on opening day. Scooping it up they walked out the front door and carefully locked it behind them.

As they were leaving, a neighbor politely inquired f they had been successful in locating whatever it was they had been looking for.

"Oh yes, thanks," said the boys, as they headed back toward the barn with its illegal elk.

AN ITINERANT CARTRIDGE

Clouds of alkali dust wafted slowly in the warm desert air as I made my way across a sage-covered dry lakebed in remote Hawks Valley in Southeastern Oregon. I was 20 miles north of the Nevada border and 60 miles from the nearest service station scouting for antelope with my sons, John and Joe. I had received an "East Beaty Two" antelope tag two weeks earlier, and I was scouting, trying to learn the lay of the land, trying to discover where and how the local antelope herds watered and fed.

I had been walking for miles. It was hot, in the low 90s, and my lips were wind burned so that I was constantly licking them to relieve their tightness. I was just scouting, but I still carried my 8MM JD Jones contender. This country is very remote, and who knows when you might run across a varmint or two.

Oregon is home to antelope, but is on the far western fringes of their range. Tags are a premium that the Fish and Wildlife only grant by a drawing once every five years. Even then, an individual is not guaranteed a tag. The rules are if you get one, you must wait five more years before applying for another. That is why I had driven 510 miles just to scout, I did not want to waste my opportunity to bag a handgun antelope. So far, I had seen three large bucks I would have been proud to bag, but I wanted to make sure I had several places to hunt when I returned in a month for the actual season. Hawks Valley is supposed to be home to the largest antelope herd in Oregon, so Hawks Valley was where I was walking.

The alkali dust was everywhere; even the jack rabbits that spooked when almost stepped on raised clouds of dust as they bounded away. Away in the distance, clouds of dust would trail out hundreds of yards and hundreds of feet high as 40 or more antelope raced to and fro trying to decide if they should run away or just a little distance as I got closer and closer. It was so remote; it was easy to picture myself as the first man to have walked on the surface of this dry lake. I knew wagon trains had traveled across it on their way to the Oregon Coast and Northern California.

With plenty of water and a large, air- conditioned Suburban awaiting me at the other side of the lake bed, I just could not imagine how difficult it must have been to have trekked across this part of Oregon with horse and wagon.

I sat down on a lump of ground to glass yet another cloud of dust. Was it a truck or more antelope? I could see it was antelope, so I spent many minutes watching to see which way they would run when leaving. Maybe, just maybe, they would leave that way when it was legal to hunt them.

The valley floor was covered not only with alkali, sage and cattle droppings, but with thousands of anthills, approximately 1 foot in height and 2 or 3 +feet across, all teeming with little red ants. As I sat and glassed, I realized what I had thought was a convenient hump of ground to sit upon was an active ant's nest as evidenced by the ants starting to crawl up my legs, biting as they moved. Jumping up, I started kicking to dislodge the little biters, but all I succeeded in doing was raising huge clouds of white dust. I wasted no time in shucking my binoculars, shoulder holster, pistol, suspenders and pants. It was the only way to get rid of the ants.

As I slowly dressed trying not to raise any more dust than necessary, I saw an old battered cartridge lying on the ground, apparently dislodged from its place in the ground by my frantic attempt to dislodge the ants. Picking it up, I naturally turned it to read the headstamp. The only problem was there wasn't any.

It appeared to be a 45-70 shell; maybe a smidgen longer, and necked. I put it into my pocket and slowly continued scouting my way to the far side of the lake. As I walked, I could not help but wonder how old the cartridge was.

Reaching back into my pocket, I took it out and again admired its battered look. I wondered who had fired it. How long had it been lying buried and hidden from the rest of the world? Had the person who fired this cartridge been after antelope or mule deer or had he been protecting his family from marauding Indians vainly attempting to drive off the white man?

But my biggest question was; what caliber is it?

I would have to wait until I returned to Coos Bay and got to Barnes' "Cartridges of the World" or Donnelly's 'The Handloaders Manual of Cartridge Conversions," to find out.

Returning home, my first chore was to thoroughly clean my Suburban, a faint white inside and out from the alkali dust. The second and more rewarding chore was to identify the cartridge I had found and wondered about for the past several days. Its overall measurements proved that my eyes were not failing. It was longer than a 45-70, not much, but a little; the differences obvious when comparing the two.

It was almost a quarter of an inch longer than a 45-70. Retrieving my micrometer, I started measuring and came up with the following: Case rimmed and bottlenecked. Length 2.25 inches. Head diameter .503. Rim diameter .595. Neck diameter .426

So what did I have? Searching through Donnelly's, The Handloaders Manual, I started with the old .45 calibers, because it looked so much like a bottle necked 45-70. No luck, so I went backwards in the.40 calibers and eventually identified it as a 40-70 Sharps necked.

In Cartridges of the World, it was described as, "This is the 40-2 1/4 inch bottlenecked Sharps that was brought out about 1876, a few years prior to the straight to the straight case. It was used in other single shot rifles, further, "The 40-70 necked cartridge had a reputation for fine accuracy and was popular as a match cartridge as much as for hunting. While many people regard Sharps rifles as strictly buffalo guns, Sharps also made match rifles that gained world wide respect on the range."

Identifying the cartridge was only the beginning. I let my imagination soar and tried to answer the questions I had asked myself earlier. How long had it lain there? Who fired it? Fired it at what? And a new question especially for those of us who are single- shot aficionados. What type of single-shot rifle was used? It had to have been one.

All in all, this entire scouting trip was a success. I saw antelope and became familiar with the territory for future hunting. I found a cartridge that had to have been fired in a single shot, and that led to my acquiring a 40-70 Sharps necked barrel for one of my Contenders. A good find, indeed.

A BLACK BEAR AND AN OLD HIWALL

The wind was steadily quartering from the southwest at a gentle two or three miles per hour, but not enough to dispel the rank, fetid odor of the rotting Holstein carcass, which bears had been feeding on for several days, but enough to make the smell barely tolerable. The western sky was turning a beautiful bright pinkish-orange as the sun slowly sank into the Pacific, and I was lying in a field near Coos River, waiting for a bear to come to the bait I had placed there several days earlier..

With my head in my arms, I was experiencing an odd sense of *deja vu*; as if I had been transported back 30 odd years in time, back to the rice paddies outside of Tuy Hoa in South Vietnam.

The mosquitoes sounded the same, and the gut-wrenching whiffs of rotten meat, (bodies) accompanied by the "whop, whop, whop" sounds of an Army reserve helicopter (a slick) hovering over a nearby ridge top, doing who knew what, at this hour of the day; probably looking for marijuana patches that can be found in this part of Oregon.

Picking up my glasses, I scanned the area where I thought the bears would be coming to feed. My 10 x 40 power Leupolds with their vast light-gathering abilities were fast becoming a necessity because of the encroaching darkness. This was the fourth consecutive night I had lain until dark and I knew if bear did not come soon, it would be impossible for me to use my Winchester

Hiwall in 50-110. The light-gathering abilities of its tang sight were pretty limited when compared to the binoculars.

Some may have considered my choice of a single-shot rifle for bear archaic, but the 300-grain Barnes bullet in its fairly large case would be potent bear medicine if one approached. The distance was just less than 75 yards and I was resting my barrel on a couple of sandbags I had packed in earlier. The sandbags would be helpful in steadying my rifle and nerves, in the event I "got bear fever". For added stability and height, I also had one of Hornady's portable plastic rests, which I had filled with sand perched on top of the sandbags.

I knew if I could see a bear, I could hit it.

Once again checking out the carcass with my Leupolds, I was amazed to see a huge, black boar bear glide into view. He had not made a sound. One second my field of view was empty. The next it was filled with this bear. Where did he come from? It was my first thought. He was not supposed to have come from the east or left, but out from under the huge myrtle tree where the carcass was lying.

The bear shuffled toward the tree, all the while sniffing the air, no doubt enjoying the very aroma that was continuing to turn my stomach. Carefully taking a bead, I placed the post of my front sight dead center in the circle of the tang on his right shoulder and slowly squeezed, all the while wondering, is there really enough light to be shooting, and am I really aiming at what I know is the shoulder? What if I am aiming too high? Too low?

"Kawham!" My 50-110 fired, spitting fire halfway across the field, and I lost sight of my bear as the recoil flipped my Winchester high into the air.

Frantically, I grabbed for my glasses, wondering, where did he go? Did I miss? Is he coming after me? Glassing, I was unable to see a thing. It was almost dark and there was not a bear in sight.

Seconds passed and then, I heard the saddest, strangest bawling sound, float up and out of the alders about 35 yards into the woods, causing shivers run up and down my spine.

I figured the bear was dead, because I had heard from other bear hunters dying bears sometimes bawl, but I have never hunted, or killed a bear and I was not sure what I had heard. I do know it was the saddest, most disturbing sound I had ever heard; a sound to raise the hairs on the back of my arms and neck and one I can still hear today.

Slowly, oh so slowly, time passed, as I waited for the recommended 15 minutes before getting up to examine the kill area. It was now dark, absolutely dark, and it was the wrong time of the year to wait for a full moon. Grabbing my flashlight, I scanned the ground, looking for signs of a hit.

Nothing. I paced and moved in ever-larger circles around the rotting carcass, while gagging on the smell. I finally found some hair and a few specks of blood. The hair was black. Was it from the bear or from the dead Holstein? I assumed it was from the bear.

Changing the lens of my flashlight from white to red, which causes blood drops to look blue, I dropped a piece of Kleenex to mark the spot, got down on my hands and knees and started looking for more blood. Every three or four feet, I found another spot and the trail made by the Kleenex pointed headed straight toward a path the bears had made as they headed into the timber.

Returning to my truck, I grabbed my United Arms Seville in 357 Maximum, and a bigger flashlight. I wanted more firepower and light before I crawled into the brush. I was wondering if I was making a mistake by tracking a black bear into a black hole on a black night. What if it was only wounded?

My anxiety level was really high as I low-crawled through the blackberries, occasionally spotting blood. I really wanted to wait until morning, when the sun would be shining and the world around me would be less fearful, but I could not. No animal deserves to be left to die a lingering death.

Deeper and deeper into the woods I crawled, shining my light up and down, left and right, looking for my bear. It seemed as if I had crawled for miles when I really knew it was only feet, but I was scared and fear can make you think funny things.

At one point, I put my hand on a huge, slimy, sticky slug and just knew I had touched the nose of my bear. Shuddering and almost screaming, I threw it aside and decided just a few yards more. If I do not find him on or near the logging road I knew was just ahead, I would wait until morning.

Reaching the old road, I spotted massive globs of blood and knew then the soulful and mournful cry I had heard, was the last sound my bear made. For just ahead, in the far reaches of my light, I could see him lying, dead.

GREENHORNS AND THEIR GREEN RIVER EXPERIENCE

Every summer, my wife Sue and I spend time together touring the back roads of America. Her objective is to find that special antique the rest of the world has overlooked and I to find that rare old rifle or pistol that a little old man wants to sell cheap. We decided this year was the year to see parts of Utah, Idaho, Montana and Wyoming.

This summer was not any different from the past; Sue did not find her special antique and I am still looking for that rare old rifle or pistol.

For several years my old college roommate Donald C. Dew has called and encouraged my wife Sue and me to fly to Utah to drift the Green River. He would spend hours telling me of his latest experiences drifting the river. He talked about the deer, sheep, bear, goats and beaver drinking and feeding along the river's banks. Wouldn't we like to have the same opportunity?

Discussing the possibility of going , Sue and I, had soon had ourselves convinced that drifting the Green River was something we should do.

So I called my friendly travel agent, and arranged for plane tickets to Salt Lake City (SLC) and a rental car, for mid-July.

Naturally the plane was late leaving Portland so we were also late leaving San Francisco. This put us into SLC about an hour behind schedule, but Don was there patiently waiting to greet us with a broad smile as we entered the concourse.

It only took a few minutes to pick up our luggage and rental car before we were headed south to Payson, Utah, where we were to visit my sister, then, spend the night at Don's sister's house.

After visiting with my sister and her family for several hours, we headed east for the ten-minute trip to our home for the night.

Don had warned us his sister and brothers-in-law were a little eccentric; the next ten hours were to prove him correct.

Arriving shortly after 9:00 p.m., we pulled up to a magnificent, newly built six- bedroom, four bath house with a, "for sale" sign posted in the driveway. The house was dark and there appeared to be someone on his hands and knees in the gravel of the front lawn. That someone stood up as we parked.

"Well, I see that you made it," was his comment as we climbed out of our cars.

"We sure did," replied Don.

"Walter I want you to meet some good friends of mine., continued Don as introductions were made.

Because it was almost dark and I noticed that Walter wearing thick kneepads and I wanted to be friendly, I couldn't help but say, "What are you doing?

"I am weeding."

"Oh, wow," I thought, "eccentric is not the word for this guy.

"Why would anyone weed in the dark, let alone weed a gravel patch?"

Things went downhill from there.

We stood outside talking for another fifteen or so minutes when Don said, "Let's go inside."

"Before you do," said Walter, "I will have to ask you to take off your shoes."

Sue and I had been forewarned by Don that we would have to remove our shoes and we understand people wanting to protect their floors and carpets.

Entering was like walking into a picture of the perfect home in, *Architectural Digest*. It was expensive, new, and everything was in perfect order.

Another fifteen minutes or so standing in the lobby talking about the house that Don's sister had gone back to visit in South Carolina, the recent drift Don had taken with Walter on the Green River just a few short weeks before. It was all idle chitchat, but I was tired and wanted to use the bathroom, get something to drink, maybe take a shower, and, most of all, find a place to sit and put my feet up after a long day of travel.

It did not happen.

By now Sue and I were making faces at one another wondering just what was going on.

Don suggested we go on a tour and look at the house.

As I told you earlier it was magnificent, but very sterile. It had highly polished oak floors placed in two foot squares, outlined in mahogany, huge chandeliers hanging from ten foot ceilings, perfect furniture and a sense that no one lived there.

As we toured, Walter would turn on one set of lights and turn off another as we went from room to room, making inane comments about how special this house was.

It was after the tour, where once again we stood around, without an offer of, "would you like to sit down?"

Still no bathroom, no offer to sit and relax and no offer of refreshments when Don asked, "Well where are we going to sleep?"

"I do not know," said Walter.

I almost laughed; here we were in a six-bedroom house and the guy did not know where we were going to sleep?

Walter went on to say, "Well we have two nice couches, one upstairs and one down that are very comfortable for sleeping."

"Great," said Don, "You guys sleep on the couches and I will bed down outside with my dog."

"That will be fine," said Sue. "Charlie, you take the couch upstairs, and I will take the downstairs one."

We had still not been invited to sit down, and visions of my sister's house with comfortable beds, showers, friendly kids, and cold fresh orange juice in the refrigerator began dancing in my head.

"What are we doing here?" I thought. "We could be in a motel."

We made the best of a funny situation.

True to his word, Don blew up his air mattress and slept on the front porch. Sue and I slept on huge, very comfortable couches.

About two in the morning, as I lay awake in a stuffy too warm room, wishing I could be sleeping outside, I realized there was not a shower in the bathroom I was told to use. I later found out Sue had asked the guy for a shower towel for her to use; and it was grudgingly provided.

Awake at five, I carefully dressed, rolled up my sleeping bag, packed my gear, and went outside for my shoes and some fresh air.

Don's bed was empty, and I saw him far up the street where it dead-ended into the sagebrush, walking his German Short hair, Bell.

I went back inside, leaving my shoes on, kissed Sue awake, and said, "Lets get the hell out of here."

"Okay. Give me twenty minutes to shower and I will be ready."

By the time Don and I returned from our short walk where we saw deer, quail and one mountain grouse, Sue had our gear packed, and we were ready to roll.

As Don was putting together his sleeping gear, Walter arrived and said, "I hope you had a restful night."

"Yes, thank you," we all chorused like school kids.

Five minutes later we were gone, headed for the Green River: No shower for me, no breakfast for us and no offer to return.

We were traveling in two cars, our rental and Don's Subaru. Two cars were needed for this trip because our particular drift of the Green River was to be 45 miles. Obviously, we had to have a way to get to the starting point to pick up car number one after our drift.

As we headed south, Sue and I chuckled about our previous night's stay and wondered aloud if Walter and his wife ever slept in the beds or if they used a couch. Sue decided they were just trying to protect their house because it was on the market for a cool million dollars.

I also told her about peeing in one of the vases, Walter's wife had on exhibit in the main living room. I rationalized it by thinking the use of the vase was better than dirtying the toilet: I'd get even for their lack of hospitality. I knew it was childish, but figured it was worth it when in a week or so they would be frantic trying to figure out where the horrible smell was coming from in their perfect house.

She was furious and horrified and berated me for minutes; until I finally admitted what I had done was wrong and apologized to her.

We continued to head south, stopping occasionally to point out places to Sue where Don and I used to hunt when we were students in Utah some 30 odd years ago. We were headed for a spot on the Green River, Ruby Ranch, and 18 miles off the highway, where we planned to start our 45-mile drift. Arriving at Ruby Ranch after driving down a dusty, wash boarded, chuck hole filled road for 45 minutes, we off loaded our gear in a manner of minutes, climbed back into the car and headed out back down the same road towards Mineral Springs where we would stash our rental car.

Getting to Mineral Springs was another adventure. It is located about 40 miles above the confluence of the Colorado and Green Rivers in Canyon Lands National Park. If you were to head to Dead Horse Point while on the road to Moab, you would drive right by Mineral Springs Road.

Mineral Springs is at the end of another 17 mile dusty, pot-hole filled road. Its final mile drops to the canyon floor by switch backing its way down a sheer cliff, so sheer, if I had been driving my ¾ ton extended cab pickup, I would have had to back and turn to make the corners.

We left our car in the sandy parking lot, climbed into Don's Subaru station wagon and headed for Moab to get our canoe.

Don's older Subaru is blessed with 4-60 air conditioning, which means roll down all the windows and go 60 miles per hour to cool off. The problem was the outside temperature was in the low 90's, so it was not long before our sweat glued us to the seats.

Arriving in Moab, we stopped at a super market that advertised a deli and bought chicken, ice and cold pop before proceeding to Tex's where Don had arranged to rent an eighteen-foot Grumman canoe.

The first thing we heard was, "Well, this is highly unusual; we do not normally rent just a canoe to individuals unless they have booked a trip with us."

You know we do not take credit cards so there is not any way we can accept a deposit to insure you just don't drive off with our canoe.

Oh well, sighed the proprietor, "Don, you have booked trips with us in the past, so I am sure our canoe will be safe."

By then I was steaming. I was hot, tired, dusty, and hungry, and all I wanted was to slip into a cool refreshing river for a quick swim. But there I stood; almost thwarted by some individual who was afraid I was going to steal his canoe. The phone kept ringing and being answered as Don and I stood patiently waiting for the clerk to tell us which canoe we could take.

Thirty minutes passed and we were still cooling our heals while the clerk explained to someone over the phone that, yes, he rented portable sealed toilets and, yes, all human waste had to be packed out, when a lady came in holding her arm, asking "Could one of you gentleman tell me how to find the hospital?"

It seems as though she had gone on one of Tex's river trips, tipped her canoe and had broken her wrist.

She was directed to the hospital, and we were taken outside, shown our canoe which they helped tie onto Don's car.

Heading north, (windows wide open) after loading the canoe and buying gas, all I could think about was how refreshing the Green River was going to feel.

Sue, Don and I had left Walter's place at 6:45 a.m. and had been on the road without a break since then. It was fast approaching 4:30, and we still had to drive back towards the town of Green River, then down the dirt road to Ruby Ranch before we could start our drift.

Finally, we arrived back at the spot where we had cached our gear earlier that morning, and I could see the river glistening through the willows and the leaves of the cottonwoods.

Dumping the rental canoe into the river, Sue started loading, as Don and I went back up the steep bank to get his canoe and gear.

It was 5:40 in the afternoon as we started our drift. I had gotten a good soaking prior to setting out, but it was not the relaxing swim I had dreamed of earlier.

When we were driving back to the embarkation point, Don

and I had discussed how difficult it is to drift when the wind blows. I shared some experiences I had had on the Rogue River, and he told me about a previous trip on the Green when the wind had blown so hard he and his partner had to camp for two days waiting for the wind to drop. But we knew the weather forecast had called for calm, cloudless days so wind would not be a problem.

However, the first thing I noticed upon starting our drift was how gusty the wind was getting. Five minutes into our drift, it was proving difficult to paddle. I remarked to Sue, that in a few minutes we will be committed to the trip because there were no take out point for the next forty-five miles.

I had no sooner made that comment when a huge gust of wind blew us backward and white caps appeared on the river's surface.

"Damn," I thought, "we are in for it now."

Taking refuge alongside the bank, we held tightly to the tamarisks to keep from being swamped by the wind. As we held tightly, the mosquitoes discovered we were in the area and within seconds we were virtually covered. Every inch of exposed skin (we were wearing shorts) was covered; our repellent was packed deep into our gear where access was almost impossible.

The mosquitoes were so bad we let go of the bushes and paddled out into the stream to get away from them.

For the next two hours we fought the wind, water, and mosquitoes as we slowly continued downstream. The scenery was spectacular: red vermilion cliffs went straight into the water on either side of us as we struggled downward into the canyon too engrossed with staying afloat to enjoy it.

By 8 p.m., we were becoming tired and looking for a place to camp. Every place that looked possible ended up being too small, steep, or impossible to get to.

By 8:30, I was getting desperate. Hollering back to Don I told him the next spot, regardless of quality, we were stopping."

Rounding a curve in the river, while cursing the wind, my sore back and my stupidity for putting Sue and me into such a mess, I spotted a patch of green on the left bank that appeared to be large enough to pitch camp.

Struggling up the muddy bank as Sue held the canoe next to shore; I found the spot was large enough for two tents and our gear. The mosquitoes also found us as we frantically unpacked, looking for bug repellent. Within seconds the air took on the gentle maddening hum that is only capable of being produced by billions of mosquitoes. So many I was reminded of a camping trip to Circle City, Alaska or the rice paddies of Vietnam.

We pitched our tents and started blowing up air mattresses as, Don made some of the nicest, coldest lemonade, I had had in years.

We skipped supper it was too miserable with mosquitoes to do anything else and crawled into our tents to rest.

I immediately discovered I had claimed the roughest, most uncomfortable ground in the tent. Imagine your air mattress stretched over three bowling balls and you might have an idea of what I was experiencing. Crawling back outside, I attempted to level the ground under the tent, and was successful to the point the bowling balls were reduced to croquet size.

Going back into the tent, I spent the next half-hour killing all the mosquitoes that had crawled in with me. The area where we were bivouacked was so small Don's tent was less than 3 feet away.

As I lay on top of my croquet balls sized rocks listening to the mosquitoes trying to get into the tent, Don started to snore. Not quiet gentle snores, but deep nose clearing gargles, and rasps that were awful to listen too.

It seemed to go on forever. Everyone, except me, was quietly sleeping, resting after an arduous day.

Three croquet balls were supporting me 4 inches off the ground, feeling miserable, tired and thirsty. "Don, Don," I yelled, "Wake up."

He stopped snoring, muttered something in his sleep, rolled over and started again.

It was a long night.

Dawn came as a gray, overcast morning, and we were up and onto the river by 5:45. I do not believe I have ever seen anyone break camp as fast as we did that morning. I thought the mosquitoes were bad the night before, but in the morning, none of us could even entertain the thought of preparing breakfast, they were so thick.

Sometime during the night I had noticed a slight haze ring around the moon, and the morning only confirmed what I had learned as a child in New Hampshire: If there is a ring around the moon, it is going to rain or snow. With 90 plus degree weather it was going to rain.

There was not any wind that early in the morning as we quietly drifted. "At last," I thought. "This is what I envisioned before leaving Coos Bay for the Green River, a peaceful drift that allowed time for communing with Mother Nature."

As Sue and I munched on plain bagels with me occasionally dipping a paddle to keep us headed downstream, I told her about the ring I'd seen around the moon the night before and that we might be in for a little rain.

The sky was cloudy, and the sun was not high enough to find its way between the steep cliffs, but we were having fun.

Roughly an hour after departing our camping site, our quiet, early morning world between the cliffs turned gray and then suddenly dark. We heard a strange roaring sound could be heard, almost as though a freight train was laboring its way upstream.

Confused about where the sound was coming from, I turned in the canoe and hollered to Don, "What's that strange sound?"

"Dunno, was his reply, "Must be the wind."

"Charlie, look," said Sue. "There on top of the cliff."

I turned to see an awesome sight. The roaring sound was rain pounding across the cliff tops, accompanied by the wind. As it reached the edge of the cliff, over our heads, the rain appeared to boil, turning into a writhing cauldron of white froth as it tried to fall, only to be tossed aloft by the winds.

Our own position on the river was no less precarious. As the wind swooped onto the surface of the river, instantly whitecaps were everywhere as we frantically paddled to shore and safety.

Reaching the safety of the bushes growing along the bank, Sue and I held on as we ducked our heads and hunched our shoulders from the rain. It was difficult not to inhale the mosquitoes that had found us in an instant, undeterred by the wind and rain as they fed on our unprotected skin.

Trying to balance my unfinished bagel on my knee, while bashing mosquitoes, and holding onto the bushes was impossible for me to do. Something had to go; and it was the bagel; overboard for fish food.

Within minutes the freak storm passed. The sky grew lighter, and the whitecaps and wind disappeared. Letting go from our sanctuary in the bushes was easy. Anything to get away from the mosquitoes, once again we were adrift on the Green River.

The rest of the morning passed uneventfully. The scenery continued to be one magnificent red cliff after another. Every bend and turn in the river opened up new vistas of beauty that we tried to capture for posterity in our minds and on film.

Noontime found us paddling onward in the face of an increasing wind so we started looking for a place to camp. Gone were the opportunities of just sitting and paddling to keep our canoe straight. By now, we had been on the water for over six hours; Sue and I were getting tired. Mosquitoes and their voracious appetites prevented us from taking refuge on shore for lunch. So, once again bagels, this time cinnamon raisin, were passed around, as well as the ever-present jug of water and we had lunch on the move.

By 1 o'clock we were barely making headway against the wind. As someone who has had two disks removed from his lower spine, I can tell you found the constant paddling was agony. Unfortunately, my only option was to continue to paddle because the sooner we got to our camping site, the sooner we could rest.

Ever since our noon bagel, Sue, Don and I had been looking for a place to quit for the day, but the cliffs rolled onward and upward, and the places to stop were once again too small, steep, or rocky.

It was 3:15 or so and my back was screaming, "Let me rest," when we rounded a curve that showed a deep canyon coming in from the left. Naturally we were on the far right side of the river hugging the bank to avoid as much upriver wind as possible, which eases paddling, when I said to Sue, "Let's go for that place."

We laboriously made our way across, and Sue held onto another limb as I climbed out of the canoe and scrambled up the slippery bank in order to do a little scouting.

Reaching the top and getting out of the bushes that lined the bank, I found a very large flat clearing, that would make a perfect campsite.

Off loading and packing our gear took a while, but soon Don,

Sue and I were scrambling around the rocks exploring. We were far enough from the river to get away from the mosquitoes and there was enough of a breeze so we did not swelter in the 100- plus degree heat radiating off the walls and canyon floor.

We soon were tired of exploring. The heat sapped our strength faster than we thought it would and our open-toed water sandals were not much protection from the rocks or-heavens forbid-the possible snake. Because of the heat, we also decided to not make camp, erect tents, inflate air mattresses or build a fire pit until the sun had gone past the cliff tops to put us in the shade.

As Don and I hauled the last of the gear to the campsite and secured our canoes for the night, Sue went looking for some shade and found it under a scraggly old juniper tree. The tree wasn't much but it cast enough shade for three people and a dog.

We spent 3 or 4 hours under the tree slowly moving around its base as the sun sank. We talked, dozed and enjoyed more of Don's ice-cold lemonade, drinking it out of tin dinner plates because we did not have any cups.

The sun finally reached the cliff tops, we started scurrying around. I scrounged firewood as Sue and Don put up the tents.

It wasn't long before we had a regular campsite with tents up, air mattresses filled and the smell of fried onions wafting in the air.

We had been on the road and river for two days. About the only thing we had eaten were bagels and fried chicken from the Moab deli. It was time for a real meal and Don had packed huge porterhouse steaks complete with a green salad and lots of fruit. As one who likes to cook over a campfire, there was no question as to who was going to cook.

I'll have to admit those medium rare steaks grilled over coals made from oak and mesquite made one of the finest meals ever consumed on the banks of the Green River.

Shortly after supper, the wind dropped and the mosquitoes moved inland trying to carry us away to wherever mosquitoes like to carry their victims.

It had been a 10-hour, 27- mile day of paddling. We were tired and went to bed.

The next morning as we embarked, dawn was a mix of riotous reds, created as the sun struck the cliff tops.

This was our last day of drifting. We had 12 miles to go before we were to take out at Mineral Springs.

The first part of the morning was pleasant; the ever –present wind came from behind giving us an added push downriver. The scenery was even more fantastic than the day before and we were able to drift alongside Don talking and chatting about the good old days.

About an hour after we had left our campsite, we caught up with a bunch of Boy Scouts in kayaks and large rubber rafts who were also heading for Mineral Springs. They had been on the river for three days and also were looking forward to rest from their incessant paddling.

By now, the winds were starting to shift, and an occasional gust would come barreling straight upstream with enough force to stop us dead in the water. It wouldn't blow long enough to push us backwards, but it was an omen of things to come.

As we paddled, listening to songbirds greeting the day, and the occasional slap of a beaver's tail striking the water in warning, I hoped the wind would stay calm enough for us to finish out our trip without having to fight it for hours on end.

Rounding a huge bend in the river, we started hearing a funny sighing sound, similar but different enough from yesterday's roar for Don to holler, "What's that noise?"

"Dunno," I hollered back. "Probably the wind."

I should have kept my mouth shout, for in minutes we were shipping white water and being pushed backwards upriver.

The next 4 hours we battled the river.

We no longer enjoyed the songbirds, the beauty of the red cliffs, or the solitude of being alone in the wilderness.

Every minute, every hour, became a struggle against the wind. We were never in real danger, but the paddling was backbreaking and very difficult.

Slowly, we made progress, and the miles and the cliffs went by as we approached our take out point.

The kayaks, being closer to the water moved ahead but never out of sight. Rounding one last curve, I spotted the kids pulling their kayaks ashore and knew we were approaching Mineral Springs.

Take-out was almost anticlimactic. The presence of so many scouts proved a blessing because they man-handled our canoes and gear out of the river faster than I could walk. Within minutes of arriving, all our gear was stacked by our rental car ready for sorting and drying and the long trip out.

The greenhorns had survived their Green River experience.